Multiple Intelligence
Approaches to Assessment

Multiple Intelligence Approaches to Assessment

Solving the Assessment Conundrum

David Lazear

Zephyr
Press
Tucson, Arizona

Multiple Intelligence Approaches to Assessment
Solving the Assessment Conundrum

Grades K–12

© 1994 by Zephyr Press.
Printed in the United States of America

ISBN 0-913705-95-0

Editors: Stacey Lynn and Stacey Shropshire
Design and production: Nancy Taylor
Cover art and design: David Fischer
Illustrations: John W. Reedy

Zephyr Press
P.O. Box 66006
Tucson, Arizona 85728-6006

Library of Congress Cataloging-in-Publication Data
Lazear, David G.
    Multiple intelligence approaches to assessment : solving the
assessment conundrum / by David G. Lazear.
      p. cm.
    ISBN 0-913705-95-0
    1. Intellect.   2. Intelligence tests.   3. Educational tests and
measurements.   4. Psychological tests.   I. Title.
BF431.L4322   1994
153.9'3—dc20   94-216

A good assessment instrument can be a learning experience. But more to the point, it is extremely desirable to have assessment occur in the context of students working on problems, projects, or products that genuinely engage them, that hold their interest and motivate them to do well. Such exercises may not be as easy to design as the standard multiple-choice entry, but they are far more likely to elicit a student's full repertoire of skills and to yield information that is useful for subsequent advice and placement.

—Howard Gardner
Multiple Intelligences: The Theory in Practice

Contents

Assessment Forms

Foreword

We are only now entering the modern age of education in which we tailor learning to suit the learner instead of making students adapt to necessarily narrow teaching styles and methods. And nowhere is that shift in honoring the many different intelligences more necessary than in the realm of assessment in which a "one-size-fits-all" view of testing has dominated education since medieval examination days. David Lazear has written another fine book that will greatly help teachers make the shift toward more tactful and insightful assessment. The material that follows is extraordinarily rich, providing a teacher with dozens of ideas on how to document and assess student performance in a probing but learner-friendly way. David Lazear has taken Howard Gardner's ideas and made them accessible to every teacher. We need more thoughtful resource books of this kind.

Grant Wiggins
Director of Research and Programs
Center on Learning Assessment and
School Structure (CLASS)
Geneseo, New York

Preface

Writing this book was almost like having an out-of-body experience. The manuscript had a life of its own. It started as a magazine article on assessment, but as I wrote, it became longer than an article, so I thought it would become a contribution to an educational journal. It kept expanding, however, until it was beyond what would be appropriate for a journal. Then I thought about publishing it as a pamphlet. And before I knew it, I had a full-blown book on my hands!

In many ways, my decision to write this book was fueled by the concerns and frustrations of the many teachers, principals, and district personnel who attend the staff development workshops I conduct on multiple intelligences. These people are generally very excited about a multiple intelligences approach to education and the difference it can make in the lives of students. But regardless of how excited they are, there is always a big question that enters our discussions: "BUT HOW DO WE ASSESS THIS KIND OF LEARNING?" (for it obviously doesn't fit into any of our current standardized testing practices). I believe answers to this question may be the missing links in the full implementation of some of the school restructuring implied by multiple intelligence theory.

My greatest concern is that this book will be used out of context—that the cart will be put before the horse. I sympathize with educators who are desperate for new directions and answers regarding assessment, for we know that much of what we are doing is destructive to students, teachers, and schools and that it works against the very aims we are after in public and private education in this country.

Nevertheless, I believe that a multiple intelligence approach to assessment should grow naturally out of a multiple intelligence approach to curriculum (teaching *for* multiple intelligences), a multiple intelligence approach to instruction (teaching *with* multiple intelligences), and a multiple intelligence approach to the learning process (teaching *about* multiple intelligences). We must overcome our tendency to go after the quick fix, the easy answer, the latest idea. The changes I suggest will not happen as a result of a one-day in-service or a four-day training program. Multiple intelligence–based assessment will be easy to implement as we restructure our schools and districts step by step so that we are teaching *for, with,* and *about* multiple intelligences. When this happens, a multiple intelligence approach to assessment will be a natural outgrowth of everything else we are doing. Otherwise, it will simply be another imposition that creates more frustration.

Never before in humanity's long journey have we known more about teaching, learning, and the actualizing of human potential than we know today. Christopher Fry, in his play *A Sleep of Prisoners*, seems to speak directly to us as educators in the midst of a major metamorphosis:

> *The human heart can go to the lengths of God.*
> *Dark and cold we may be, but this*
> *Is no winter now. The frozen misery*
> *Of centuries breaks, cracks, begins to move.*
> *The thunder is the thunder of the floes,*
> *The thaw, the flood, the upstart Spring.*
> *Thank God our time is now when wrong*
> *Comes up to face us everywhere,*
> *Never to leave us till we take*
> *The longest stride of soul men ever took.*
> *Affairs are now soul size*
> *The enterprise*
> *Is exploration into God.*
> *Where are you making for? It takes*
> *So many thousand years to wake,*
> *But will you wake for pity's sake?*

I hope you find this book a useful resource as we continue the important restructuring dialogue and transformation process that is occurring in American education today.

Very special thanks to everyone at Zephyr Press for their patience as I completed this manuscript. I lost track of the number of times I asked them to change their deadlines to accommodate this manuscript gone out of control. Their support has been unwavering.

I again express my gratitude to Howard Gardner for his continuing work on the theory of multiple intelligences, especially at the point of practical applications he is sensing. I am also deeply appreciative of his continuing friendship, encouragement, and support of my work, a great deal of which is based on his pioneering research on multiple intelligence theory.

And finally a huge thank you to all of the upset and frustrated teachers I've encountered in workshops, seminars, and conferences across North America.

You have prodded, cajoled, and enticed me, maybe unwittingly, but nevertheless actually, into attempting to apply the theory of multiple intelligences to restructuring our approaches to assessment. Without you and your willingness to risk change on behalf of students, this book never would have been.

David Lazear
December 1993
Chicago, Illinois

Prologue

The Face of the Conundrum

Conundrum (kə-'nən-drəm)

n [origin unknown] 1. a riddle, anything that puzzles; 2a. a puzzle or problem that is usually intricate and difficult of solution; b. a question or problem having only a conjectural answer. *syn.* mystery

---

Situation 1

Mr. Devoe, a middle school science teacher, was thrilled by how well his students were learning and understanding the basic concepts of biology. They were able to apply many of the principles they had learned to a variety of situations in the lab, as well as to produce various facts when playing "Biology Jeopardy," a game he had devised to help them remember key concepts. On the standardized science test he was required to give at the end of the term, however, his students' performance was less than satisfactory. In an interview with the school principal he expressed his frustration: "I know they know the material! They have been using it and applying it on a daily basis all semester. I don't understand why they couldn't produce on the test."

Situation 2

Mr. and Mrs. Kringle were shocked by the report card their third-grade daughter, Andrea, brought home from school. She had been so excited about school and what she had been learning during the term. They felt she was not only gaining very valuable information from the various subjects she was studying, but that she was acquiring many important life skills. They had also noted significant growth and development of her knowledge and skills throughout the term. Why, then, did she bring home a report card that did not reflect any of this?

Situation 3

Chris, a high school sophomore, was depressed by the score he received on the final test in his American history class. He felt that the test wasn't fair because it did not test in the same ways as he had learned and studied the material. In the learning situation, he had been given opportunities to master the material in a wide variety of ways: in cooperative learning groups; through art, music, dance, and drama; and through more traditional learning modes. With the exception of the traditional modes, however, none of these were included on the test! Chris knew that he knew and understood the material. The written test was just too limiting and did not allow him to demonstrate the fullness of his learning.

These three scenarios perfectly illustrate what I call "the assessment conundrum"; namely, our students almost always know, understand, and have learned much, much more than they can demonstrate on any tests we must administer. And yet, we educators are required by school boards, legislatures, and taxpayers, who pay for public education, to preoccupy ourselves with getting better and better test scores each year, even when we know that these test scores do not tell the whole story of what our students have learned, what they understand, and what they know about various subject areas. In *A True Test: Toward More Authentic and Equitable Assessment*, Grant Wiggins (1989) eloquently describes the conundrum we are facing: "When an educational problem persists despite the well-intentioned efforts of many people to solve it, it's a safe bet that the problem hasn't been properly framed. Assessment in education has clearly become such a problem since *every state reports above-average scores on norm-referenced achievement tests and since everyone agrees (paradoxically) that such tests shouldn't drive instruction but that their number and influence should nonetheless increase."* (emphasis mine)

Rarely do we question the validity and meaning of test scores, and so they tend to control how we approach public education today. I am not against standardized tests as such, as long as we understand that the scores we get are only one small piece of the information we have about our students' actual intellectual capabilities and knowledge of a subject.

Not all progress is scientifically quantifiable. Our current reliance on test scores as the measure of both one's intelligence and one's academic success assumes both that human beings can be labeled and categorized based on a series of decontextualized, paper-and-pencil exercises and that learning can be reduced to a mechanical process with clear-cut goals and definable outcomes, much like the process of producing a car on an assembly line in Detroit. In a booklet entitled *The Portfolio Approach to Assessment,* Emily Grady (1992) states,

> The desire to know in quantifiable terms exactly what our students have learned is a peculiarly American trait, but there seems to be little correlation between testing and producing successful students. American students are among the most tested yet academically deficient in the industrialized world. According to many educators and psychologists—even the head of Educational Testing Service—standardized tests just do not pass muster as a method of improving student performance. In fact they may be undermining the very purpose they were intended to serve.

This addiction to test scores wrongly assumes that all students are (or should be) the same. Also, our standardized tests are blatantly biased against some students who are not particularly skilled at the art of test-taking.

In fact, high scores on tests often reveal little more than which students are good at taking standardized tests. And all too often our competency as educators is judged solely on the basis of how our students perform on "objective" tests. One of the things that drove me to write this book was a conversation I had with a high school English teacher in a workshop I was conducting. This man is as committed a teacher as you could hope to find. He has a solid understanding of the learning process, of effective instructional practices (which apply state-of-the-art, research-based teaching techniques in the classroom), and of the psychology of high school students. What is more, he loves teaching and genuinely likes working with teenagers. Nevertheless, I had before me a frustrated and nearly defeated man. Several things he said in our conversation have haunted me for some time:

I feel like a mere technician whose job is to prepare students for tests rather than a skilled professional whose role is to facilitate the learning process and to unlock the vast learning potentials and intellectual capabilities of my students.

Sometimes I feel like the war criminals at the Nuremberg trials must have felt. I know that what I am doing [relative to current assessment practices] is destructive to my students, both in terms of their self-esteem and their learning. And yet, I've got to follow the orders I'm given to get higher and higher test scores. To a great extent, my evaluation as an educator, by my administrators, peers, and community, to say nothing of my salary level, rests mainly on this.

I got into the teaching profession because I wanted to serve the needs of the next generation of Americans by providing them with the skills and knowledge they would need to function effectively and successfully in the world. Who am I in fact serving? College admissions officers, school board policy-makers (whose major concerns are often more political than in the best interests of students), district schedule-makers, school board/district budget committees, and secretaries who want a simple formula for entering grades into computers. Why do all of these concerns take precedence over the needs of students?

Where do our state legislators come up with their "mandates" for school reform? Do they even have a clue what goes on in schools today and who the student population is? Do they know that the world has changed from when they went to school, and that therefore schooling, which is supposed to prepare students to live effectively in this new world, must be different, as well? How many of them are even marginally aware of the most up-to-date educational research on effective teaching, learning, and human development? I feel like we (students and teachers alike) are often nothing more than pawns in their political chess games.

In an article that appeared in *Educational Leadership,* Carl Glickman (1991) summarizes this teacher's frustrations and the moral dilemma as follows:

For too long, professionals have gone about the business of teaching and operating schools in ways they privately admit are not in the best interests of students. The reasons for doing so are plentiful—we all live with district policies, state regulations, traditional school structures, mandated curriculum alignment, community pressures, and limited resources. . . .

We must confront our knowledge and use it to guide our efforts; then we must operate our schools in different ways, using our knowledge. . . . We [must] ask that the school be the center for professional decisions where teachers and administrators control the priorities and means of helping students to learn.

This book is about confronting our knowledge and applying it to restructuring the assessment process in our schools. In so doing, I believe that assessment can become a profound means for enhancing and deepening the learning of our students and for giving back to teachers the *raison d'être* that led most of them to enter the vocation of being a professional educator.

1

An Emerging New Paradigm of Assessment

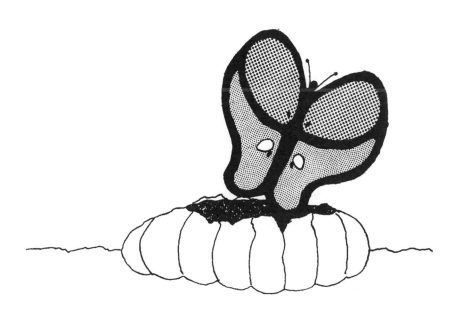

I believe that something like a paradigm shift is happening in education today. American physicist and historian of science Thomas Kuhn (1962) popularized the concept of paradigm shift in his classic work *The Structure of Scientific Revolutions*. In science, a paradigm is a conceptual system or worldview that dominates people's thought and perception. A paradigm clearly defines what is "real" and what cannot be real in a given culture or era. It identifies legitimate problems, offers methods for solving them, and provides various screens or eyeglasses for evaluating and interpreting various data and experiences. For example, the accepted paradigm in the Middle Ages placed Earth at the center of the universe. This worldview controlled what people actually saw when they gazed at the heavens and what was considered acceptable in philosophical and theological speculation. In another period, the "flat Earth" paradigm provided the boundary for people's imagination and thinking.

Any questioning of the assumptions of the accepted paradigm is usually discouraged or, at best, not supported. Data and experiences that challenge the dominant view are often suppressed or ignored. As it becomes more and more difficult to disregard elements or ideas that just don't fit into the dominant paradigm, however, what Thomas Kuhn calls a "paradigm crisis" develops.

According to Kuhn, when it is no longer possible to disregard "anomalies" or to fit them into the old worldview, the situation is ripe for a shift to a new paradigm. Kuhn (1962) describes the dynamics of this shift:

> Normal science ultimately leads only to the recognition of anomalies and to crises. And these are terminated, not by deliberation and interpretation, but by a relatively sudden and unstructured event. . . . Scientists often speak of the "scales falling from the eyes" or of the "lightning flash" that "inundates" a previously obscure puzzle, enabling its components to be seen in a new way that for the first time permits its solution. On other occasions the relevant illumination comes in sleep. No ordinary sense of the term "interpretation" fits these flashes of intuition through which a new paradigm is born. (122–23)

The old and new paradigms at first seem to represent entirely different and conflicting worldviews. What actually happens, however, is a subsuming of the insights of the old paradigm within the new, emerging paradigm, which results in a dramatic transformation in perspective and subsequently in practical living.

Part of the catalyst for the paradigm shift that I suggest is under way in American education is the theory of multiple intelligences. This theory presents us with a new understanding of human intelligence and learning and thus is a pivotal point for a dramatically new understanding of the potential of students. Many key discoveries in research have contributed to the shaking of the foundations of all our previous understanding of human intelligence, or in the language of Kuhn, have created sufficient anomalies that we are experiencing a paradigm crisis:

- **Intelligence is not fixed or static at birth.** In the past, we thought that one's intelligence was more or less determined by heredity and could be assessed through tests yielding a quantifiable intelligence quotient (IQ). The IQ, we thought, would reveal what an individual's intelligence capabilities were. This idea of fixed intelligence, however, did not take into account the wide variety of environmental, cultural, and socialization factors that affect the development of intellectual capacities. Many researchers now feel that we may have defined intelligence too narrowly and that it is a far more flexible and plastic phenomenon than we previously thought. In fact, these researchers are now looking at intelligence as a set of capabilities that are continually expanding and changing throughout one's life!

■ **Intelligence can be learned, taught, and enhanced.** Because intelligence capabilities have a neurobiological base, almost any mental ability can be improved at any age. There are many kinds of exercises one can perform to strengthen and enhance intelligence skills, much like what we do to improve and expand any other skill (parallel parking, making a pie crust, performing a jackknife dive). Generally, the more we practice the better we become. We can learn to be more intelligent in more ways and on more levels of our being than we ever thought possible!

■ **Intelligence is a multidimensional phenomenon that is present at multiple levels of our brain/mind/body system.** There are many ways in which we know, understand, perceive, learn, and process information. Howard Gardner, co-director of Harvard University's Project Zero, coined the phrase *multiple intelligences* to describe these multi-knowing capacities. His research suggests that we all possess at least seven types of intelligence, or seven ways of knowing. Moreover, he believes there are probably others that we have not yet been able to test.*

These findings are directly challenging the assumptions on which the current assessment paradigm rests. In the wake of this shift in our understanding of intelligence and human potential, a dramatically new paradigm of assessment is rapidly emerging. Let us try to catch a glimpse of this paradigm shift, even as we are in the midst of it.

---

* Phi Delta Kappa granted permission to reprint this section from *Teaching for Multiple Intelligences,* Fastback pamphlet #342, published by Phi Delta Kappa Educational Foundation.

Logical-Mathematical Intelligence

The knowing that occurs through the process of seeking and discovering patterns and through problem solving. It uses such tools as calculation, thinking skills, numbers, scientific reasoning, logic, abstract symbols, and pattern recognition.

Verbal-Linguistic Intelligence

The knowing that occurs through the written, spoken, and read aspects of language as a formal system. It uses such tools as essays, debates, public speech, poetry, formal and informal conversation, creative writing, and linguistic-based humor (riddles, puns, jokes).

Visual-Spatial Intelligence

The knowing that occurs through seeing both externally (with the physical eyes) and internally (with the mind's eye). It uses such tools as drawing, painting, sculpture, collage, montage, visualization, imagination, pretending, and creating mental images.

7 Ways of Knowing*

Bodily-Kinesthetic Intelligence

The knowing that occurs through physical movement and performance (learning by doing). It employs such tools as dance, drama, physical games, mime, role-play, body language, physical exercise, and inventing.

Intrapersonal Intelligence

The knowing that occurs through introspection, metacognition (thinking about thinking), self-reflection, and "cosmic questioning" (What is the meaning of life?). It uses such tools as affective processing, journals, thinking logs, teaching for transfer, higher-order thinking, and self-esteem practices.

Interpersonal Intelligence

The knowing that occurs through person-to-person relating, communication, teamwork, and collaboration. It employs such tools as cooperative learning, empathy, social skills, team competitions, and group projects that foster positive interdependence.

Musical-Rhythmic Intelligence

The knowing that occurs through hearing, sound, vibrational patterns, rhythm, and tonal patterns, including the full range of potential sounds produced with the vocal chords. It utilizes such tools as singing, musical instruments, environmental sounds, tonal associations, and the endless rhythmic possibilities of life.

* Adapted from *Seven Ways of Knowing: Teaching for Multiple Intelligences* by David Lazear (Palatine, Ill.: Skylight, 1991).

The Old Assessment Paradigm	The New Assessment Paradigm
All students are basically the same and learn in the same way; therefore, instruction and testing can be standardized.	There are no standard students. Each is unique; therefore instruction and testing must be individualized and varied.
Norm- or criterion-referenced standardized test scores are the main and most accurate indicators of student knowledge and learning.	Performance-based, direct assessment, involving a variety of testing instruments, gives a more complete, accurate, and fair picture of student knowledge and learning.
Paper-and-pencil tests are the only valid way to assess academic progress.	Student-created and maintained portfolios, which include paper-and-pencil tests as well as other assessment tools, paint a more holistic picture of students' progress.
Assessment is separate from the curriculum and instruction; that is, there are special times, places, and methods for assessment.	The lines between the curriculum and assessment are blurred; that is, assessment is always occurring in and through the curriculum and daily instruction.
Outside testing instruments and agents provide the only true and objective picture of student knowledge and learning.	The human factor, that is, people subjectively involved with students (for example, teachers, parents, and the students themselves), holds the key to an accurate assessment process.
There is a clearly defined body of knowledge that students must master in school and be able to demonstrate or reproduce on a test.	Teaching students how to learn, how to think, and how to be intelligent in as many ways as possible (that is, creating lifelong learners) is the main goal of education.
If something can't be objectively tested in a uniform and standard way, it isn't worth teaching or learning.	The process of learning is as important as the content of the curriculum; not all learning can be objectively tested in a standardized manner.

The Old Assessment Paradigm (continued)	The New Assessment Paradigm (continued)
The student is a passive learner, an empty receptacle to be filled.	The student is an active and responsible learner, and thus a partner with the teacher in the learning process.
Curriculum and school goals are to be driven by tests and test scores.	Curriculum and school goals are to be driven by a desire to tap the full intelligence and learning potential of students.
The Bell curve, used to sort students into categories of successful, average, and failing (on a given test on a given day), is a reliable assessment of students' knowledge and abilities.	The J curve is a reliable assessment of students' knowledge and abilities, for it shows the growth of knowledge and abilities in a compounding fashion.
Monomodal testing practices (verbal-linguistic and logical-mathematical, that is, "reading, writing, and 'rithmetic") are the only viable means of testing students.	Multimodal testing practices based on the multiple intelligences (including visual-spatial, bodily-kinesthetic, musical-rhythmic, interpersonal, and intrapersonal, as well as verbal-linguistic and logical-mathematical) are all viable means of testing students.
Educators should use a behaviorist model to understand human development.	Educators should use a humanistic/developmental model to understand human development.
All students should be tested at the same time, using the same testing instruments, which are evaluated using the same criteria, giving educators a way to compare and contrast a student's achievement with that of other students.	Students are at varying developmental stages; testing must therefore be individualized and developmentally appropriate and should provide educators with information about how to reach and teach them more effectively, producing students who are more successful more of the time.

The Old Assessment Paradigm (continued)	The New Assessment Paradigm (continued)
The efficiency of an assessment approach (that is, easy to score, easy to quantify, easy to administer) is the paramount concern when developing tests.	The benefits to students' learning is the paramount concern when developing tests; efficiency is not an issue if assessment serves the needs of students and helps them improve their lives.
Assessment should be used to point out student failure, make comparisons among students, and rank students to determine their "standing" in the school.	Assessment should be used to enhance and celebrate student learning, to deepen understanding, and to expand their ability to transfer learning to life beyond formal schooling.
Teaching and learning should be focused on curriculum content and acquiring data.	Teaching and learning should be brain compatible and focused on the learning process, the development of thinking skills, and understanding the dynamic relationships between curriculum content and real life.
Academic progress and success should be measured using traditional, predetermined, standardized criteria and instruments.	Academic progress should be measured using current, research-based educational practices that take into account individual needs, differences, and cognitive and psychological factors.
Learning is the mastery or understanding of various bits of objective, factual information such as dates, processes, formulas, figures, and so on.	Learning is first and foremost a subjective affair in which one's understanding of self and world is transformed, expanded, questioned, deepened, upset, stretched, and so on.
Successful teaching is preparing students to achieve on various tests designed to assess their knowledge in different subjects.	Successful teaching is preparing students for effective living throughout their lives; it therefore focuses on "teaching for transfer" of learning beyond the classroom, into one's daily living.

Running through this paradigm are several motifs that not only call into question current assessment values, practices, and philosophy, but also ask us to redefine the very meaning of being human today.

Individual Student and Teacher Differences

We are as different from each other as snowflakes, and we must take these differences into account when we are looking to restructure our schools. Just because a student does not perform well on a written or standardized test does not mean he or she lacks an understanding of certain concepts. Not all students know, understand, and learn in the same way. We must honor these differences if we are to gain an accurate picture of students' learning and help them succeed in school. If we are genuinely concerned to reach all students and teach them things they need to succeed in the larger world, we must put an end to the assembly line approach to assessment and testing. As I mentioned earlier, there are no standard kids. We must stop trying to create them! We must stop kidding ourselves that the full story of a student's development can be told by administering various standardized tests. Yes, written, standardized tests do tell a part of the story, BUT ONLY A PART!

Of course, what this obviously means is that both instruction and assessment must become highly individualized to meet the unique learning needs and personalities of each student. Will this approach be more time consuming? Of course. Will it be more complex? Most certainly it will. But do we owe it to the students who are in our care? Most definitely, for it will give us a far more accurate picture of our students and thus reveal to us how we can better serve them. Most people who chose to become professional educators did so because they wanted to help students. Most were concerned to provide future generations with the knowledge and skills needed to live effectively. Whether we realized it or not, when we made the decision to enter this vocation, we also implicitly entered a covenant with all children who enter our classrooms, to help them realize their full intellectual potential. Our vocation carries with it the responsibility to beckon, coax, stimulate, cajole, and spur all students to step beyond their limits and realize their full potential as human beings.

The same things can be said of teachers. Not all teachers teach most effectively in the same way. And yet, often, the standards by which we evaluate teachers are static, narrow, rigid, and simply unfair, given the wide variety of instructional strategies, techniques, tools, and approaches teachers need to reach all students. We expect all teachers to measure up to certain pre-established teaching criteria, including written lesson plans that follow specified planning formats (which may have no relationship to the actual "eventfulness" of truly creative teaching and learning), classroom behaviors or conduct that meet certain artificially imposed standards of discipline (which may have little or no relationship to what it takes to create an optimal learning environment for students), and comparative analyses of students' performance on a wide variety of standardized tests (which reveal a very small portion of a student's full grasp of a given subject area).

Teachers must be evaluated and held accountable for their teaching, just as any provider of service in our society. But why not use evaluation criteria similar to those we use elsewhere in society? When we hire a carpenter to build an entertainment unit in our house, we evaluate the work based on the final product. When we hire a lawyer, we evaluate the performance on what the lawyer accomplishes on our behalf. Why, therefore, should we not evaluate teachers by the final product they produce: the students who are in their care? If our evaluation of teachers is to be fair, we must look at much more than standardized test scores can reveal. We must look at such things as students' thinking and learning skills; their intellectual, emotional, and social development; their capacity to transfer and apply classroom learning to life in the real world; and their creative problem-solving abilities. Why not begin now to evaluate teachers based on their capacity to produce these results, even if the way they way they get them does not fit into the more traditional modes of instruction? These are the criteria by which their students will be evaluated one day in the workplace.

Developmentally Appropriate Education

Jan and Dave Ulrey (1992), national consultants who specialize in the implementation of developmentally appropriate practices, make the following observation about a multiple intelligence approach to the classroom learning and teaching situation:

> *Developmental learning recognizes that children grow and develop as a whole, not one dimension at a time or at the same rate in each dimension.* Therefore, there is an understanding that children learn through active involvement using instructional practices that address the social, emotional, physical, aesthetic, and intellectual needs of children. The theory of multiple intelligences provides the framework for this idea.
>
> *In a developmental classroom, the awareness of different learning styles and intelligences is a key factor in both the development of the curriculum and the choice of instructional strategies.* Teachers value the "whole" child, focus on the strengths of each individual, and provide learning experiences which stimulate growth in the seven intelligences. (4–6; emphasis mine)

In chapter 2 of this book, I attempt to provide some initial guidelines for evaluating the developmental aspects of students' intelligence. Far more important than the specifics of these guidelines, however, is the understanding that every student is a unique and unrepeatable being who deserves the chance to be treated and evaluated as such. In my own teaching I have adopted the practice of evaluating myself and my own teaching practices far more than I evaluate a particular student. I have a conversation with myself that goes something like this: "Okay, what I'm currently doing isn't working. What could I do that would reach this student? What does this student like? What are his or her strengths? What doorways, other than the one I'm currently using, could I come through that would reach him or her?"

Multiple Intelligence Approaches to Assessment © 1994 Zephyr Press, Tucson, Arizona

I hold as a fundamental belief that there is no such thing as an "unreachable" student. The task is mine, not the students', to find the pathways to turn them on to learning. And I also have discovered that acutely observing students involved in various activities and learning tasks will teach me everything I need in order to reach them. In chapter 3 I present some of the observation instruments I have found to be effective in this task, and in chapter 4 I offer some suggestions of strategies and techniques to help all students become active, responsible learners.

A Holistic Picture of Human Beings

Part of the problem with our current assessment practices is that they provide, at best, very superficial and limited information about the full potential of our students. Human beings are far more complex and more profound than can be accurately measured by any standardized assessment tools or instruments. And yet, children are often categorized and labeled early in their schooling based on their performance on various intelligence, ability/skill diagnostic evaluation instruments; these labels include LD, gifted, special ed, at risk, attention deficit disorder, highly capable learners, hyperactive, and so on. Unfortunately, students tend to believe that they fit into these categories and under these labels. Thus the labels often tend not only to become self-fulfilling prophecies for students in school, but they also limit teachers' and parents' vision of students and their capabilities, both in school and at home. And what is worse, these labels often follow one throughout life.

Of course, the second problem with current standardized testing practices is that they tend to be biased toward verbal-linguistic and logical-mathematical intelligence, with a smattering of visual-spatial thrown in for interest. And even the visual-spatial aspects of tests are often seen as "handmaidens" to verbal-linguistic intelligence. In fact, as a culture, we often feel that "real learning" has occurred only when someone can score well on a written test. While such testing may be an efficient way of assessing student learning, it is unfortunately grossly inaccurate, prejudiced against alternative (but nonetheless valid) ways of knowing. And such tests are blatantly unfair to students who may not know, understand, perceive, and learn in the so-called traditional reading, writing, and arithmetic ways.

We also often make the mistake of not paying attention to students' feelings about what they are learning, their capacity to integrate and apply what they learn in school to situations beyond the classroom, and the impacts on the development of their self-concept and understanding.

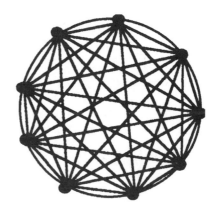

What if we were simply to redefine the standards of standardized testing to include at least seven intelligences? What if we gave equal value to the development of a full range of human capacities and skills, including visual-spatial, bodily-kinesthetic, musical-rhythmic, interpersonal, and intrapersonal, and stopped favoring verbal-linguistic and logical-mathematical skills? What if we provided parents with a picture of a whole child in the reports we send home, giving in our reports dynamic, developmental profiles of children, as opposed to norm- or criterion-referenced, quantity-based scores? What if we were to create assessment instruments that valued the subjective aspects of one's learning equally with the mastery of certain so-called objective facts?

What if we did testing that helped students make the transfer of learning? Implementing these suggestions would not only move us in assessment directions that are more aligned with the emerging new assessment paradigm, but they would also get the human factor back into our assessment practices; that is, assessment would be focused on enhancing learning, amplifying self-understanding, and expanding students' full intellectual development.

The Importance of Process vs Content

We are living in the midst of what has been called a "knowledge explosion." Some researchers have suggested that our "knowledge base" changes at a rate of 80 percent every five years. In light of these vast changes, we must raise serious questions about what we should be teaching in our schools. The old Chinese proverb about giving someone a fish, which feeds a person for a day, or teaching someone how to fish, which feeds a person for a lifetime, is brought to mind by this situation. Should we be concerned primarily with students' learning particular bits of information that will likely change several times by the time they graduate from high school? Or should we be more concerned with teaching them how to learn?

As we move to redefine standards and expectations in our schools, we must be sure they are broad enough to include the full spectrum of intellectual development of our students. This education must include, but not be limited to, the mastery of specified bits of knowledge that our society values as well as the processes that make one capable of lifelong learning, even when (and maybe especially when) specific knowledge explodes or changes right before our eyes!

I do not mean to downplay the importance of mastering academic content, because the learning and thinking process is a parasite: it must have some*thing* to learn and to think about! I mean simply that content should not be the main focus. Such things as knowing how to use or apply the content and understanding the dynamic relationships of the content should be paramount. I think we need to spend as much time teaching students how to be creative thinkers and problem solvers; how to meet challenges; and how to adapt, transfer, and integrate the content they learn in school into the task of daily living as we do asking them to memorize various bits and pieces of information.

In the pages that follow I attempt to present a new operating, practical vision of assessment that is aligned with the emerging new paradigm. Chapters 2 through 4 deal with new approaches to the so-called intelligence testing or ability testing of students. These chapters address assessing students' relative strengths and abilities in the different intelligence areas, and then using this information to reach and teach them more effectively. In the models I suggest, the approach is to come through the doorway of a student's strength and ability and use the strength to train or empower a weakness.

Chapters 5 through 7 deal with new approaches to assessing and evaluating students' academic progress. These chapters describe practical models that can broaden the scope of current testing practices, which are based almost exclusively on verbal-linguistic and logical-mathematical intelligences. The models and techniques I suggest in this section present approaches for using assessment to enhance, deepen, and expand students' learning rather than pointing out their failures. The ultimate goal of the book is to help us serve the educational needs of *all* students more adequately and thus to help more students succeed more of the time in our schools.

2

Seven Ways of Knowing

A Developmental Perspective

(Theoretical Background)

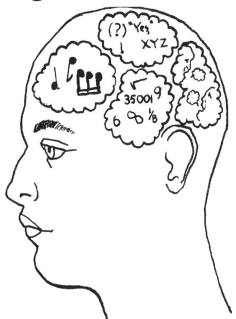

Timmy, a third-grade student, was not doing very well in all the parts of school that count. His teacher reported, "He seems not to be interested in anything we do in class. In fact, I often catch him doing things other than the work I have assigned students to do, and he talks to other students and distracts them, as well." His daily written work was far "below average." He was frequently in the principal's office for a variety of dicipline problems. In consultation with Timmy's parents, his teacher decided that he needed a diagnostic evaluation to see if Timmy had a learning disability.

A series of tests administered by a learning specialist psychologist from the district revealed, to no one's surprise, that Timmy indeed had a number of learning disabilities, including attention deficit disorder and dyslexia. As a result of this diagnosis, to everyone's relief except Timmy's, he was pulled out of the regular classroom and placed in a special education class for remediation of these so-called disabilities.

The Old Paradigm: A Deficit-Based
Approach to Intelligence Testing

I believe that the number one assessment issue and challenge we are facing in American education is that most of the assessment we do, both intelligence testing and the assessment of academic progress, is deficit based; that is, we come at the process of assessment from a negative, weakness, disability standpoint, as illustrated in the story about Timmy. In fact, most instruments by design ferret out failure, ineptitude, and weakness. In intelligence testing (or "diagnostic evaluation" as it is currently called), where our goal is to assess students' intellectual abilities and aptitudes, the deficit base ultimately leads us to affix various kinds of labels to students (attention deficit disorder, gifted, behavior disordered, and so on). This labeling is generally based on the results of a student's performance on various standardized, criterion-referenced intelligence, cognitive, and psychological testing instruments, which purport to give us "objective information" about intellectual abilities. Thomas Armstrong (1987) makes the following important observation about the myth of objective testing in his book *In Their Own Way:*

> The tester . . . may unintentionally manipulate the child's behavior for good or ill. Already having some idea of why the child has been referred for evaluation, he carries a subliminal set of expectations concerning how the child will perform. This works against the child referred for learning problems, since the tester will be on the lookout for any signs of difficulty and may unconsciously reinforce wrong answers or fail to give the child opportunities to perform well.
>
> Whatever the outcome, it's clear that these assessments do not objectively test a child's ability. As San Diego University sociologist Hugh Mehan . . . and his colleagues also observed, . . . learning disability specialists use a "test until find" approach in their work, where testers administer assessments to a child until they locate a suspected disability—at which point they stop testing and label the child. If they don't locate a disability after two or three tests, they administer up to fifteen or twenty other tests until they either find a disability or exhaust their entire battery. This way of working with children encourages fault-finding and minimizes the chances of discovering strengths and abilities. (30–31)

Of course, several problems occur anytime we label other human beings: First, the label usually limits our vision of who they are and of their possibilities. We decide for them what they are capable or incapable of and usually don't even give them the chance to try, let alone work with them to improve their abilities in, a given area. A second problem is that the labels often become self-fulfilling prophecies for the labeled person, and others may see only what the label suggests; that is, not only does one tend to accept the label and live out of it, so to speak, but those within one's sphere of influence tend to reinforce the label, generally without ever questioning its validity. Third, the labels we give children in elementary school usually stick with them throughout their formal schooling and often follow them well into their adult lives.

The nature of the conundrum may be seen no more clearly than at this point. We know that this kind of testing and labeling of students is damaging to them and yet at the same time, in many cases, schools can receive almost twice as much funding from federal and state governments for the "learning disabled" child as for the "normal" child. Nevertheless, we must stop labeling students! Thomas Armstrong (1993) says, "I prefer not to use the label learning disabilities because people tend to identify too strongly with the term. There's a certain quality of fatalism that accompanies the label—the idea that it's somehow an indelible part of one's learning life rather than something that can be transformed. Instead I like to think of these weak links as learning difficulties or even learning opportunities because they can challenge one to new heights" (171).

Something I said earlier bears repeating here: *There are no standard kids! So why are we so fixated on standardized ability and intelligence tests?* Each of us is unique and unrepeatable. We are far more complex, mysterious, and profound than any standard testing instrument can reveal. Most tests also have built into them blatant cultural, ethnic, and class biases. We must stop labeling children (or any human being) because labeling is simply an unfair practice. In *Multiple Intelligences: The Theory in Practice,* Howard Gardner (1993) makes the following point:

> Now a huge body of experimental evidence exists to indicate that assessment materials designed for one target audience cannot be transported directly to another cultural setting; there are no purely culture-fair or culture-blind materials. Every instrument reflects its origins. . . . There is also an accumulation of findings about the cognitive abilities of various kinds of experts. It has been shown that experts often fail on "formal" measures of their calculating or reasoning capacities but can be shown to exhibit precisely those same skills in the course of their ordinary work. . . . *In such cases, it is not the person who has failed but rather the measurement instrument which purported to document the person's level of competence.* (172; emphasis mine)

During the first twenty years of my professional life, I worked with an international human development organization. One of the experiences this work afforded me was living and working for about five years on Chicago's West Side. As I look back on this experience, I am shocked and amazed by the number of students I encountered who were brilliant in "street smarts" (that is, highly developed inner-city survival strategies) but who were nonetheless labeled as special ed or learning disabled. The current biases of our Western systems of education do not value the kinds of highly intelligent behavior these students exhibited.

In almost every staff development workshop that I conduct, teachers and administrators relate at least one story about a student who is highly skilled in various areas that are not valued by our current curriculum and assessment practices. I hear stories about students who are mechanically brilliant—able to disassemble and assemble a machine with no set of written instructions; students who are natural comedians; students who can draw anything you ask them to; students who are "human relations marvels"; the so-called weird, self-reflective students who often don't fit in with the rest of the children; students whose performances are brilliant on the playground in a sports game; and . . . The examples could go on and on. In most cases, these students are falling through the cracks of our present educational system simply because we don't value these dimensions of personhood, the students don't test well, and they don't fit into the mold of current definitions of intelligence. In these cases, the question Gardner raises is important food for thought: Who has really failed here? The student or the test?

Another part of the problem with criterion-referenced ability tests is that they generally occur out of context, that is, in a situation not typical of the situations in which these abilities would be used in real life. Grant Wiggins (1989) describes this dilemma: "That is why most so-called 'criterion-referenced' tests are inadequate: the problems are contrived, and the cues are artificial. Such tests remove what is central in intellectual competence: the use of judgment to recognize and pose complex problems as a prelude to using one's discrete knowledge to solve them" (706).

Thomas Armstrong (1987) makes a similar observation and discusses some of the longer range effects of these tests on children as well as the implications for our schools and potentially for the larger society:

> These diagnostic tests—like their kin the intelligence and achievement tests—have little to do with the real lives of children. . . . Most of these tests demand that children do things they've never done before, would never choose to do on their own, and will never do again. Yet on the basis of their performance, these tests classify children as either normal or disabled learners. . . .
>
> [Diagnostic] tests do a disservice to the deeper emotional needs of these youngsters, and serve the needs of the test makers instead. For, by manufacturing disability in the assessment room, test makers are creating a whole new generation of "disabled" individuals who must now have their problems "remediated" by fancy educational programs, often created by the test makers themselves. (29, 30)

We must find new ways to catalyze, evoke, pull out of, or otherwise cajole students to reveal the full range of their intellectual capacities, especially those students who don't fit into our current definitions and understanding, and especially if they aren't "testable" by our current methods. We owe it to our students to create whole pictures of who they are as human beings, and then to use this information to help them master the various academic disciplines involved in gaining a formal education.

Teaching Intelligence: The Developmental Levels Defined

As I mentioned earlier, one of the key findings of contemporary intelligence research is that intelligence can be taught, learned, developed, and enhanced. At any age and at almost any ability level we can learn to be more intelligent, in more ways, and on more levels of our brain/mind/body system than we ever thought possible before. In my view, this means that we should not only be constantly on the lookout for intelligent behavior that the system may be missing, but we should also be continually looking for ways to help students stretch into new intellectual areas—maybe areas in which they are uncomfortable or weak. In order to be effective in this approach, we need to understand the unique developmental pathway each intelligence takes so that we can design developmentally appropriate practices to help students learn to meet their full intellectual potential. In general each intelligence develops in a hierarchical fashion. We move from the "novice" level to the "mastery" level, which we often see in people who have chosen vocations or various avocational pursuits that rely on particular intelligences and require high levels of skill development in a particular area. The general developmental template could be mapped as follows.

Basic Level

This is the developmental level that generally occurs during infancy and early childhood. Much of what develops during this stage is a result of early socialization factors. We learn many basic capacities and skills of the intelligences from family, friends, and our environment, stimulating the development of our intelligences.

Complex Level

This developmental level most often occurs during the elementary school years. This is the period in which we try to build on the basic skills we learned during early childhood and to expand our intellectual repertoire. Educators' concerns should be not only to increase the number of skills students have at their disposal, but also to increase their faculty in using a variety of intelligence strategies for problem solving, meeting challenges, and gaining and mastering the knowledge we are seeking to impart in our educational system.

Coherence Level

Often this developmental level is the focus of secondary education. During this stage our goal is generally to prepare students for life in the "real world." What this means is that our educational concern should shift from learning and expanding skills and capacities to teaching students how to integrate the skills into normal patterns of living beyond the formal educational setting. Our concern here should be with refining students' proficiency in using their varied intellectual capacities as well as teaching them when and how to employ most effectively the different intelligences in the tasks of daily living.

At this point it is important to say that, although the intelligences tend to develop in a somewhat systematic manner, with certain capacities and skills developing before others, this may or may not be related to the chronology of one's educational journey. The levels I have described are only general guidelines to assist us in designing developmentally appropriate practices within a formal educational system. They are not meant to be used to label or categorize students. There are obviously many striking examples of young children who can perform so-called coherence-level intelligence skills and who have developed the capacities I am suggesting. This developmental schema in no way suggests hard-and-fast stages based on age or educational level, nor does it suggest rigid grade level, skill-based curriculum development.

When working with the intelligences, be they seven or seventy, we must greatly individualize instruction and assessment and be deeply sensitive to individual uniqueness and needs. The Intelligence Capacities Inventory Wheel from *7 Pathways of Learning* (see figure 1) can assist us in tracking the development of the various intelligence capacities and skills in individual students as well as giving parents intelligence development reports on their children to enlist their support in helping children tap their full intellectual potential.

The Intelligence Development Pathways: A Foreword (and Disclaimer)

One of the problems that exists in trying to create a developmental picture of the seven intelligences is that, from a neurological perspective, all of the intelligences are interrelated and, in normal people, tend to operate in a well-orchestrated, integrated manner. Therefore, it is impossible to isolate an intelligence or look directly at it. However, we can understand some of what is involved if we look at what Howard Gardner calls the "developmental trajectory" of the various intellectual capacities. I am suggesting that these capacities tend to evolve from basic to complex to coherence levels. The charts that follow are designed to help us gain a general picture of the development of specific intellectual capacities, which I have, for the sake of understanding, categorized under the different intelligences. The truth of the matter is, however, that if we are interested in seeing a particular intelligence at work, we must look at combinations of intelligences as they operate within certain domains or special projects, such as conducting a scientific experiment, performing a drama, illustrating a book or story or poem. All of these activities require many capacities from all of the intelligences, which work in concert with each other to complete the given task.

Multiple Intelligence Approaches to Assessment © 1994 Zephyr Press, Tucson, Arizona

Figure 1. Multiple Intelligence Capacities Inventory*

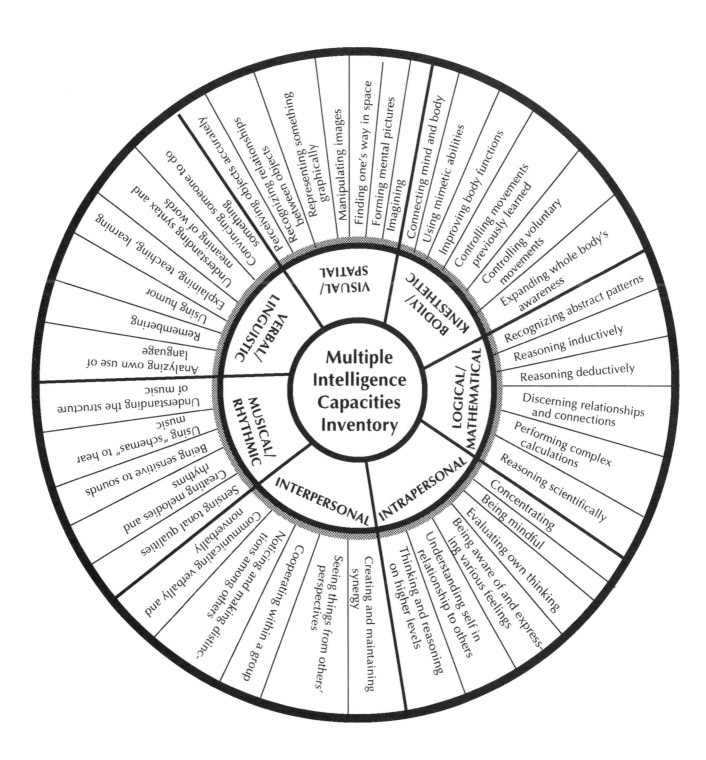

* Adapted from David Lazear's *Seven Ways of Knowing: Understanding Multiple Intelligences* (Palatine, Ill.: Skylight, 1991).

A second issue is that some of the intelligence capacities can occur at each of the developmental levels and could logically fit under more than one intelligence. So, for example, although humor is listed as a capacity of verbal-linguistic intelligence, it can be convincingly argued that each intelligence has its own special and unique form of humor, albeit not linguistically based. What I am suggesting is that by developing one's capacity to grasp such linguistically based humor as puns, jokes, twists of the language, and riddles, one's verbal-linguistic capacities are enhanced. However, this is not to suggest that the manifestation of these capacities will occur exclusively or even primarily in the language arts. We must look for the manifestation of the various intelligence capacities in many different areas and then use this information to help students develop the full spectrum of their intelligence capacities. Chapter 4 gives some ideas, gathered from a range of activities, for using such observations of how the capacities manifest themselves to amplify and enhance the learning of students who exhibit a variety of intelligence profiles (intelligence profiles are discussed in chapter 3).

The assessment of students' intellectual development and ability level is important given the brain/mind research that shows that intelligence is not fixed and static at birth! It is a far more flexible, changing, expanding phenomenon than we used to think. At least one of the implications of this new understanding is that once we have a picture of students' relative strengths and weakness, their interests and disinterests in the various intelligence areas, we have new information to help them realize and develop the full spectrum of their intellectual capabilities. This information can likewise assist us in designing developmentally appropriate teaching and learning practices for our schools as well as guide us in creating intelligence integrated curricula in which students are taught how to use and strengthen all of their intelligences in and through the curriculum.

Following is an initial attempt to define some benchmarks of the developmental pathway for each of the seven intelligences. After each developmental chart are suggestions for evaluating and ascertaining students' intelligence capacity development. We are obviously dealing not with a one-shot evaluation here but with a process that continues throughout the year and, I hope, throughout students' educational careers.

Likewise, there are a number of evaluative criteria that could (and should!) be applied to the capacities I have suggested at each of the developmental levels. In this writing, I have focused the sample evaluation reports on the assessment of interest in the different capacities. However, using the same format, we could also evaluate the development of skill in using the different capacities. Screening in this way is important because often something in which we exhibit a great deal of strength and skill is something in which we have very little interest. The reverse is often the case as well; we may find ourselves very interested in and drawn to something for which we have not as yet exhibited or developed much skill. Still another evaluation criterion that should be applied to the capacities is one's predisposition to use certain capacities when left to one's own devices, one's "comfort zone," frequency of use, and ease of utilization. These kinds of additional criteria can potentially give us not only a fuller understanding of our students and their unique intelligence developmental journeys, but also help us in the creation of individualized, intelligence-appropriate opportunities to assist students in reaching their full intellectual potential.

Note: The evaluation reporting formats that follow each chart are adapted from the experimental report cards of the Harmon Elementary School (Las Vegas) and the assessment research of the Gloucester Spectrum Project. (See appendix for examples of these reporting instruments.)

Verbal-Linguistic
Capacities Developmental Journey

Basic Skill Level

(involves acquisition and basic development of "building block" language arts capacities, including simple reading and writing, and rudimentary patterns of speaking)

- knowledge of the alphabet (that is, ability to recite and recognize various letters)

- recognition of one's own name in writing and in conversation

- single word utterances; speaking pairs of words and meaningful phrases

- creation of simple sentences, generally with poor syntax, in speaking

- ability to perform "imitation writing," especially of one's own name and other letters

Complex Skill Level

(involves understanding various aspects of language as a system, for example, grammar, syntax, phonetics, and praxis, and the development of language comprehension skills)

- complex and proper use of language to communicate ideas, desires, and feelings

- capacity to tell jokes and understand various kinds of language-based humor (jokes, puns, and so on)

- expanded vocabulary, including skill in using new words in speaking and writing

- execution of self-initiated writing to communicate thoughts, opinions, feelings, and so on

- comprehension of information presented in a written format (stories, narratives, and so on)

Coherence Level

(involves development of the creative and self-expressive dimensions of linguistic communication and expanded comprehension and interpretive capacities)

- self-expression in various creative writing forms (essay, poetry, narrative, and so on)

- ability to create original stories and to relate classical and previously heard stories

- execution of various types of formal speaking (debate, persuasive, impromptu, and so on)

- skilled use of various figures of speech (metaphor, simile, hyperbole, and so on)

- ability to engage in meta-linguistic (language investigating itself) analysis and dialogue

Multiple Intelligence Approaches to Assessment © 1994 Zephyr Press, Tucson, Arizona

Verbal-Linguistic
Capacities Development Evaluation

(1=low interest; 2=consistent growth; 3=high interest)

Basic Level

	1	2	3
knowledge of the alphabet			
recognition of one's name			
single word/phrase speaking			
creation of simple sentences			
skill in "imitation writing"			

Complex Level

	1	2	3
skilled communication			
telling/understanding humor			
expanded vocabulary usage			
self-initiated writing			
comprehension of reading			

Coherence Level

	1	2	3
self-expression in writing			
creating/relating stories			
skilled formal speaking			
use of figures of speech			
meta-linguistic analysis			

NOTES

Logical-Mathematical Capacities Developmental Journey

Basic Skill Level

(involves development of simple concrete object manipulation skills, concrete pattern recognition, and the ability to perform simple abstract thinking)

- capacity to perform concrete object manipulations based on specific criteria

- ability to count and perform basic sequencing tasks (for example, putting things in an order)

- recognition of numbers and being able to relate number symbols to concrete objects

- competence to engage in simple abstraction involving concrete objects

- recognition of simple, concrete cause-and-effect relationships

Complex Skill Level

(involves learning a variety of problem-solving processes, effective thinking patterns, and standard mathematical calculation skills and operations)

- ability to perform a range of standard mathematical operations and calculations

- grasp of a variety of problem-solving skills and possible approaches

- development of a variety of thinking patterns and knowing how to use them

- ability to engage in abstract thinking based on conceptual information

- understanding of various mathematical processes and logic patterns

Coherence Level

(involves development of advanced mathematical process skills and operations, as well as integrated, application-oriented thinking, including the transfer of learning)

- competence in linking various mathematical operations for complex problem solving

- knowledge of how to find unknown quantities in a problem-solving situation

- understanding and utilizing a variety of metacognitive processes and behaviors

- performance of logical thinking and standard math proofs

- ability to engage in both inductive and deductive reasoning processes

Multiple Intelligence Approaches to Assessment © 1994 Zephyr Press, Tucson, Arizona

Logical-Mathematical Capacities Development Evaluation

(1=low interest; 2=consistent growth; 3=high interest)

Basic Level

	1	2	3
concrete object manipulations			
basic sequencing/counting			
recognition of numbers			
simple abstraction			
cause/effect relationships			

Complex Level

	1	2	3
standard math operations			
problem-solving approaches			
utilizing thinking patterns			
abstract thinking (conceptual)			
mathematical processes/logic			

Coherence Level

	1	2	3
linking math operations			
finding unknown quantities			
metacognitive processes			
logical thinking/math proofs			
inductive/deductive reasoning			

NOTES

Visual-Spatial Capacities Developmental Journey

Basic Skill Level

(involves learning the skills for engaging in sensorimotor curiosity about the world and for exploring manipulatively and spatially one's environment)

- recognition of, enjoyment of, and response to a variety of colors

- recognition of, enjoyment of, and response to a variety of shapes

- creation of simple drawings, patterns, shapes, images, and designs

- physical manipulation of objects and assembly of things with the hands and fingers

- movement from one location to another (crawling, walking, and so on)

Complex Skill Level

(involves learning more structured, formal, and disciplined approaches to the visual arts and the ability to understand spatial relationships and locality)

- recognition of and ability to reproduce spatial depth and dimension

- reproduction of scenes and objects through drawing, sculpting, and painting

- understanding how to read maps, including legends, distance, and other symbols

- use of the active imagination, ability to form mental images, and pretending

- ability to see, recognize, and understand objects or scenes from different perspectives

Coherence Level

(involves an integrated use of visual-spatial capacities to solve problems, deepen understanding, express oneself, and expand creative thinking)

- understanding how to make something from a blueprint, pattern, or diagram

- accurate map-making to give directions and symbolize aspects of a location

- impressionistic and expressionistic creation of art forms

- understanding of abstract spatial images (for example, geometry)

- recognition and creation of complex visual-spatial relationships and patterns

Multiple Intelligence Approaches to Assessment © 1994 Zephyr Press, Tucson, Arizona

Visual-Spatial
Capacities Development Evaluation

(1=low interest; 2=consistent growth; 3=high interest)

Basic Level

	1	2	3
color discernment			
shape discernment			
drawings, patterns, designs			
object manipulation, assembly			
basic spatial movement			

Complex Level

	1	2	3
spatial depth, dimension			
drawing, sculpting, painting			
map reading, understanding			
imagination, mental images			
various perspectives			

Coherence Level

	1	2	3
understanding blueprints			
accurate map-making			
visual art form creation			
abstract spatial imagery			
complex pattern, relationships			

NOTES

Bodily-Kinesthetic Capacities Developmental Journey

Basic Skill Level

(involves learning and developing basic motor skills that range from automatic reflexes to intentional movement for the purpose of attaining certain individual goals)

- execution of various automatic physical reflexes such as sucking, reaching, turning head

- performance of simple motor skills such as turning over, standing, sitting

- doing a variety of activities to gain physical independence such as crawling and walking

- performance of various actions to achieve control of the environment

- implementation of a variety of goal-oriented actions to get what one wants

Complex Skill Level

(involves development of more complex levels of physical movement along with progressive degrees of coordinated body movement)

- utilization of various appropriate expressive gestures and body language

- development of coordinated motor skills (dance, roller skating, riding a bike, and so on)

- ability to role-play or perform charades to communicate various situations

- enjoyment of physical challenges, sports games, and body exercise routines

- successful performance of hands-on creation tasks or projects

Coherence Level

(involves learning to use the body as a vehicle of expression of ideas, feelings, beliefs, and values as well as developing genuine skill in the physical use of the self)

- ability to perform in a variety of creative invention activities or to make something new

- creative and expressive body movements (for example, "refined body language," drama)

- enactment of complex scenes that show ideas, values, and concepts (for example, mime, role-play)

- execution of complex physical movement routines (for example, gymnastics, dance)

- skilled execution of goal-oriented physical movements (for example, sports games)

Bodily-Kinesthetic Capacities Development Evaluation

(1=low interest; 2=consistent growth; 3=high interest)

Basic Level

	1	2	3
automatic physical reflexes			
simple motor skills			
physical independence			
environment-control actions			
goal-oriented actions			

Complex Level

	1	2	3
gestures, body language			
coordinated motor skills			
role-play, charades			
body exercise routines			
hands-on creation tasks			

Coherence Level

	1	2	3
invention activities			
expressive body movements			
enactment of complex scenes			
complex physical movements			
goal-oriented movements			

NOTES

Musical-Rhythmic Capacities Developmental Journey

Basic Skill Level

(involves learning to recognize, respond to, and produce basic patterns of music and rhythm, as well as developing associations with musical-rhythmic sounds)

- recognition of and response to a variety of tonal patterns and sounds

- ability to reproduce or mimic a variety of specific tones and sounds

- recognition of and response to a variety of rhythmic patterns and beats

- ability to reproduce or mimic a variety of specific rhythms and beats

- emotional associations with various sounds (tones and rhythms)

Complex Skill Level

(involves developing an awareness of music and rhythm as expressive media as well as learning to enjoy music and rhythm and understanding their impact on oneself)

- ability to produce different kinds of melodies and songs (both original and learned)

- awareness of the impact and effects of various kinds of music and rhythm

- matching various music and rhythm with one's feelings or moods

- enjoyment of a variety of music types and specific rhythms or beats

- ability to produce different kinds of rhythms and beats (both original and learned)

Coherence Level

(involves appreciation for music and rhythm both as a formal system and as a medium of communication with others, as well as creative expression of oneself)

- competence in using music and rhythm to express ideas, thoughts, and feelings

- ability to create and share one's sense of music with others

- recognition and understanding of different musical forms and rhythmic patterns

- comprehension of the "language of music" (for example, musical symbols and terms)

- appreciation for and understanding of different kinds of music and rhythms

Multiple Intelligence Approaches to Assessment © 1994 Zephyr Press, Tucson, Arizona

Musical-Rhythmic Capacities Development Evaluation

(1=low interest; 2=consistent growth; 3=high interest)

Basic Level

	1	2	3
recognition of tones, sounds			
reproduction of tones, sounds			
recognition of rhythms, beats			
reproduction of rhythms, beats			
associations with sounds			

Complex Level

	1	2	3
production of melodies, songs			
awareness of music's impact			
matching feelings and music			
enjoys various music, rhythms			
production of rhythms, beats			

Coherence Level

	1	2	3
expressing ideas in music			
sharing music with others			
recognition of musical forms			
understanding music's language			
appreciating variety of music			

NOTES

Interpersonal
Capacities Developmental Journey

Basic Skill Level

(involves developing fundamental familial relationships and learning the basic skills of person-to-person relating, including communication and acceptance of others)

- establishment of meaningful bonds and relationships with parents and siblings

- recognition, acceptance of familiar others (for example, extended family and family friends)

- development of simple communication strategies with others

- ability to imitate sounds, words, and facial expressions made by another person

- development of basic "compromise/agreement strategies"

Complex Skill Level

(involves learning the skills of human relating that go beyond the family, including the social skills of cooperation and collaboration with other people)

- establishment of meaningful peer relationships that go beyond the family

- development of effective social skills of cooperation and collaboration

- ability to empathize with others and to understand their perspectives/ viewpoints

- comprehension of factors involved in being an effective member of a team

- ability to participate in various situations of complex social role-playing

Coherence Level

(involves a thorough understanding of group dynamics, human relations, basic human social behavior, and an appreciation for cultural and individual differences)

- ability to build consensus in a group situation or effectively manage or resolve conflict

- comprehension of various group dynamics strategies and group process factors

- understanding processes and methods of cooperative or group problem solving

- sensitivity to individual differences in perspective, beliefs, motivations, and so on

- appreciation for varying cultural values and norms and social ideals

Multiple Intelligence Approaches to Assessment © 1994 Zephyr Press, Tucson, Arizona

Interpersonal Capacities Development Evaluation

(1=low interest; 2=consistent growth; 3=high interest)

Basic Level

	1	2	3
meaningful family bonding			
recognition of familiar others			
communication strategies			
imitation of another			
complex "social role-playing"			

Complex Level

	1	2	3
meaningful peer relationships			
effective collaborative skills			
empathy with others			
being an effective teammate			
basic "compromise strategies"			

Coherence Level

	1	2	3
builds consensus in a group			
understands group dynamics			
group problem-solving skills			
grasps individual differences			
appreciates cultural variety			

NOTES

Intrapersonal Capacities Developmental Journey

Basic Skill Level

(involves development of simple self-awareness, skills of basic independence, and a genuine curiosity about oneself and the world)

- awareness and expression of a variety of personal feelings and moods

- ability to associate different emotions/feelings with specific experiences

- consciousness of the "I" or the existence of a "self" separate from mother/family

- exhibition of movements toward and desire for self-independence

- asking why and trying to make sense out of one's world/environment

Complex Skill Level

(involves acquiring skills of self-reflection, self-understanding, and self-esteem, including the ability to "step outside of the self" and reflect on one's thinking, behavior, moods)

- development of skills of concentration, focusing the mind

- growth in individual self-esteem and appreciation for one's uniqueness

- concerned with acquiring various self-improvement skills

- ability to define and understand the whys of personal likes and dislikes

- understanding of how one's own behavior affects other's relationship to the self

Coherence Level

(involves expanded development of the skills of introspection, including metacognition, self-analysis, mindfulness, personal beliefs, values, and philosophies)

- ability to express oneself through the creation of various kinds of symbols

- ability to control one's own emotional states, feelings, and moods

- involved in an active identity search (for example, asking "Who am I?")

- exploration of and forming personal beliefs, values, goals, and philosophies

- conscious use of higher-order thinking/reasoning processes in problem-solving situations

Multiple Intelligence Approaches to Assessment © 1994 Zephyr Press, Tucson, Arizona

Intrapersonal Capacities Developmental Journey

(1=low interest; 2=consistent growth; 3=high interest)

Basic Level

	1	2	3
awareness of feelings, moods			
feeling, experience associating			
conscious of "I"/separate self			
self-independence actions			
"why" questioning			

Complex Level

	1	2	3
skills of concentration/focus			
regard for self's uniqueness			
"self-improvement" skills			
understanding personal tastes			
grasping one's behavior effects			

Coherence Level

	1	2	3
self-expression in symbols			
conscious emotional control			
active "Who am I?" quest			
forming personal philosophy			
use of higher-order thinking			

NOTES

What About Report Cards?

Although I am not suggesting sending parents report cards as detailed as the intelligence development evaluation reports outlined here, I do believe that it is possible to send home reports that give parents a relatively complete and holistic picture of their children's intellectual development.

Most of the report cards we now send home emphasize development in the areas of verbal-linguistic intelligence and logical-mathematical intelligence. I am not suggesting that we stop reporting on these areas. I am suggesting, however, that to report *only* on these intelligences and not to report *equally* on the development of the other intelligences gives a very unfair picture of all that is happening to a child in school and of what she or he may be gaining from the educational journey. Although school boards, state legislators, parents, and the general public tend to be biased in favor of verbal-linguistic and logical-mathematical development, often at the expense of the development of the other intelligences, there is nothing preventing us from creating reports that give the traditional reading, writing, and arithmetic information *as well as* the larger story of children's full intellectual development. I have included several report cards in the appendix as examples of how some schools are approaching such reporting.

Some additional report card ideas could include the following:

- **Why not ask parents to send a report card from home to school?** These report cards could serve as periodic reports on children's development and the various things parents are learning about their children as the parents watch the children play, perform various tasks around the house, converse during meals, and so on. Parents know many things about their children and their children's intelligences that could help educators more effectively teach the children in school.

- **Why not ask students to do a self report card?** This report card could match the report card you send home but with students grading themselves in the same categories. There should be space for them to write any explanation they feel is necessary, as well as space (*and encouragement*) to add to the self report card categories that they feel give a more adequate picture of their progress.

- **Why not let students create peer report cards for each other?** These report cards would be especially effective when students have been doing extensive work in cooperative groups. Each member of the group would create a report card for the other members, using predetermined and understood categories. This activity could also work if you have students work with partners at the end of a term, review the work they did during the term, and write formal reports on what they sense about their partners' progress. The report should include both great successes of the term as well as areas that need work.

I believe that if we are to serve deeply the learning needs of our students and help them reach their full intellectual potential in their educational journey, then we must take into account anything and everything that helps us better understand the whole person we are trying to teach.

3

Intelligence and Ability Testing Revisited

Creating Student Intelligence Profiles (Models for Change)

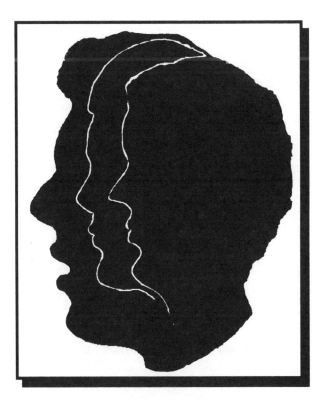

In my first book, *Seven Ways of Knowing,* I briefly discussed Howard Gardner's concept of creating intelligence profiles for our students and suggested that creating them should be the main goal of intelligence testing: "The assessment of intellectual profiles remains a task for the future. We believe that we will need to depart from standardized testing. We also believe that standard pencil-and-paper, short-answer tests sample only a small proportion of intellectual abilities and often reward a certain kind of decontextualized facility. The means of assessment we favor should ultimately search for genuine problem-solving or product-fashioning skills in individuals across a range of materials" (Gardner 1983).

Gardner suggests that what we really need from intelligence testing is not a score that represents a decontextualized picture of how a given student performed on a given test on a given day; instead we need an individual's "intelligence profile" at a given time in her or his life. This profile is not static; it is a dynamic reflection of one's growth and development. A profile would show both strengths and weaknesses along with ways to develop an individual's intelligence capacities to the fullest extent possible. In the early years of schooling, the profile could help discern ways of developing each student's full spectrum of intelligences. In the later years, the profile could be used to help point students in the directions of particular vocations for which they have exhibited an aptitude and an interest.

Gardner suggests further that it should be possible to gain a reasonably accurate picture of a student's intellectual profile over the period of about a month of careful observation of that student involved in various activities and learning tasks. Gardner (1983) says, "The total time spent might be five to ten hours of observation—a long time given current standards of intelligence testing, but a very short time in terms of the life of that student." I do not think Gardner necessarily means five to ten hours per student; this kind of observation can happen as we learn to watch our students in groups while they are engaged in various activities, at play, and in various learning situations.

In *Seven Ways of Knowing* I presented five "student watch" techniques to assist teachers in observing students through the eyeglasses of multiple intelligences. Following is an expansion and revision of these techniques along with suggestions for how to score, record, understand, and interpret the observations made in these various activities. The key to these assessment tools is to remember that no single tool tells the whole story of a student's intelligence capabilities. Rather, many instruments are needed that, together, will give us an indication of what makes a given student tick intellectually.

The need for this kind of intelligence assessment is underscored in *Teaching and Learning through Multiple Intelligences* by Linda Campbell, Dee Dickinson, and Bruce Campbell (1992). These authors discuss one of the findings of Project Spectrum at Harvard University, the early childhood assessment project based on Howard Gardner's multiple intelligences research:

> In assessing the individual intelligences, Project Spectrum researchers discovered the importance of considering the "working styles" of children as they interact with materials or tasks of a specific kind of intelligence. Some students demonstrate the working style across several intelligences, while the styles of others appear influenced, in part, by the tasks at hand . . . Working styles refer to the processes of learning and may provide insight into approaches to tasks that may help or hinder learning. (200)

There are, of course, certain disciplines, interdisciplinary areas, and curricular domains in which this observation of the multiple intelligences at work may be relatively easy. For example, staging a play, designing "applied math" projects, conducting and reporting on a scientific experiment, producing a product in industrial or home arts classes, and creating historical simulations potentially can engage all seven intelligences. In such learning activities, the key is to carefully watch students involved in the act of creation and to record your observations about their employment of various intelligence capacities/skills. The "Inventing" student watch instrument on page 65 provides a way to do this kind of observation. Also, in chapter 7 I have presented a variety of other "domain" projects, performances, displays, and exhibitions that potentially can help us "catch them being intelligent" in more informal ways than the more formal "student watch" instruments that follow. The key is to find a variety of student watch techniques that are most comfortable for you and that are a good fit with your current instructional practices and techniques.

Student Behavior Log

Procedure

Create a list of behaviors to watch for in students as they are involved in a variety of learning tasks and activities. Observe them over a three- or four-week period, watching for consistent behavior patterns. These clear patterns may give you clues on how a student processes information in a lesson.

Student Behavior Log

Student Name: _____

Age: _____ **Date of Observation:** _____

Indicate the degree to which you observe the stated behavior or characteristic in each student using the following scale: 0 = uncertain; 1 = does not fit at all; 2 = fits slightly; 3 = fits moderately; 4 = fits strongly

Verbal-Linguistic Behaviors
Loves talking, writing, and reading almost anything	0	1	2	3	4
Precisely expresses her- or himself both in writing and talking	0	1	2	3	4
Enjoys public speaking	0	1	2	3	4
Is sensitive to impact of words and language on others	0	1	2	3	4
Understands and enjoys plays on words and word games	0	1	2	3	4

Logical-Mathematical Behaviors
Is good at finding and understanding patterns	0	1	2	3	4
Is quick at solving a variety of problems	0	1	2	3	4
Can remember thinking formulas and strategies	0	1	2	3	4
Likes to identify, create, and sort things into categories	0	1	2	3	4
Is able to follow complex lines of reasoning and thought processes	0	1	2	3	4

Visual-Spatial Behaviors
Frequently doodles during class activities	0	1	2	3	4
Is helped by visuals and manipulatives	0	1	2	3	4
Likes painting, drawing, and working with clay	0	1	2	3	4
Has a good sense of direction and understanding of maps	0	1	2	3	4
Creates mental images easily; likes pretending	0	1	2	3	4

Bodily-Kinesthetic Behaviors
Has difficulty sitting still or staying in seat	0	1	2	3	4
Uses body gestures and physical movement to express him- or herself	0	1	2	3	4
Is good in sports; is well-coordinated physically	0	1	2	3	4
Likes to invent things, put things together and take them apart	0	1	2	3	4
Likes to demonstrate to others how to do something	0	1	2	3	4

Musical-Rhythmic Behaviors
Hums quietly to her- or himself while working or walking	0	1	2	3	4
Taps pencil, foot, or fingers while working	0	1	2	3	4
Can remember songs and rhymes easily	0	1	2	3	4
Likes to make up tunes and melodies	0	1	2	3	4
Senses musical elements in unusual or nonmusical situations	0	1	2	3	4

Interpersonal Behaviors
Has an irresistible urge to discuss almost everything with others	0	1	2	3	4
Is good at listening and communicating	0	1	2	3	4
Sensitive to the moods and feelings of others	0	1	2	3	4
Is a good, effective team player	0	1	2	3	4
Is able to figure out the motives and intentions of others	0	1	2	3	4

Intrapersonal Behaviors
Is highly intuitive and/or "flies by the seat of pants"	0	1	2	3	4
Is quiet, very self-reflective and aware	0	1	2	3	4
Asks questions relentlessly; has avid curiosity	0	1	2	3	4
Is able to express inner feelings in a variety of ways	0	1	2	3	4
Is individualistic and independent; is not concerned about others' opinions	0	1	2	3	4

Multiple Intelligence Approaches to Assessment © 1994 Zephyr Press, Tucson, Arizona

Student Behavior Log Scoring
(adapted from the work of Frank Rainey)

1. Begin by transferring the numbers from each intelligence behavior observation to column A on the table below.

VERBAL-LINGUISTIC:

—— ——
—— ——
—— ——
—— ——
—— —— ——
A   B   C

MUSICAL-RHYTHMIC:

—— ——
—— ——
—— ——
—— ——
—— —— ——
A   B   C

LOGICAL-MATHEMATICAL:

—— ——
—— ——
—— ——
—— ——
—— —— ——
A   B   C

INTERPERSONAL:

—— ——
—— ——
—— ——
—— ——
—— —— ——
A   B   C

VISUAL-SPATIAL:

—— ——
—— ——
—— ——
—— ——
—— —— ——
A   B   C

INTRAPERSONAL:

—— ——
—— ——
—— ——
—— ——
—— —— ——
A   B   C

BODILY-KINESTHETIC:

—— ——
—— ——
—— ——
—— ——
—— —— ——
A   B   C

---

2. Multiply each response value in column A as follows and record the result in column B:

   If response = 0, multiply by 0.   **If response = 3, multiply by 2.**
   If response = 1, multiply by 0.   **If response = 4, multiply by 3.**
   If response = 2, multiply by 1.

3. Average column B for each intelligence and record the average in column C (round to the nearest whole number).

4. Turn to the "Multiple Intelligences Profile Indicator" on page 71 and graph the average score by darkening the appropriate segment(s) for each intelligence area.

Note: Any average score that is greater than 4 should be plotted as 4+ on the wheel.

Student Behavior Log

Notes and Reflections

Intelligence Skill Games

 ## Procedure

Set up a series of intelligence game stations or centers around the classroom. Explain what is in each station, then let students choose which station they want to go to. Watch students as they play the games over a period of several weeks. Let them choose which games to play, but encourage them to try games from each of the stations. Note which games are their favorites. Carefully observe students in the act of playing the various games and note how they play the games.

Intelligence Skill Games

Student Name: _____

Age: _____   **Date of Observation:** _____

Verbal-Linguistic Games

Spelling games, such as crossword puzzles, word jumbles, Scrabble™,
  or Spill and Spell™
Word guessing and vocabulary games, such as hangman and balderdash
Impromptu speaking games, such as drawing an object from a bag
  and giving a speech about it
Linguistic twist games, such as riddles, pun wars, or "Can you top this?"
  joke telling

Logical-Mathematical Games

Strategy games, such as Clue™ and Monopoly™
Logical and numerical pattern games, such as Rummycube™
Card games, such as Old Maid™, go fish, or Rook™
Logical thinking and remembering games, such as Trivial Pursuit™

Visual-Spatial Games

Games that require seeing patterns, such as checkers, chess,
  Rubick's Cube™, and tic-tac-toe
Graphic representation games, such as Pictionary™ or connect-the-dots pictures
Imaging games, such as jigsaw puzzles or "What's wrong with this picture?" games
Games that require following spatial directions, such as scavenger hunts or
  map-reading challenges

Bodily-Kinesthetic Games

Role-playing and mime games, such as charades
Motor-coordination and balance games, such as Twister™ or
  creating human pyramids
Body language games, such as mirroring a partner's movements or
  expressing emotions
Multitracking games, such as jogging in place, snapping your fingers,
  and blinking all at the same time

Musical-Rhythmic Games

Music recognition games, such as "Name That Tune"
Music creation games that begin with "Create a song about . . . "
Rhythmic patterns and sound recognition games that begin with
  "Guess what made this sound"
Rhythmic pattern and sound creation games, such as "Going on a Lion Hunt."

Interpersonal Games

Noncompetitive games and activities, such as those in *Playfair* by Joel Goodman
  and Matt Weinstein
Communication games, such as gossip or joint storytelling
Human interest guessing games, such as "What's My Line?" or "I've Got a Secret"
Working together in team games, such as relay races

Intrapersonal Games

Exploring one's values games, such as Scruples™
Self-analysis games, such as surveys and questionnaires
Mind expansion games, such as brain teasers or complex visualization journeys
Creativity games, such as those suggested in Roger van Oeck's
  A Whack on the Side of the Head

Intelligence Skill Games Scoring

(adapted from the Gloucester Spectrum Project)

Instructions

1. For each intelligence area, record your observations of *how* students play the game by circling the appropriate number on the following chart:

ENGAGEMENT *(level of involvement)*

0	1	2	3	4
very low	low	moderate	high	very high
(refusal to play)	(resistant)	(passive; no initiative)	(eager; invested)	(focused involvement)

COMFORT ZONE *(level of confidence)*

0	1	2	3	4
very low	low	moderate	high	very high
(resists; seeks assurance)	(hangs back)	(unsure participation)	(at ease)	(sure of self; skillful)

ENJOYMENT *(level of positive and negative effects)*

0	1	2	3	4
very low	low	moderate	high	very high
(no delight; tense)	(rigid; businesslike)	(little expression)	(playful; pleased)	(shows obvious delight)

UNDERSTANDING *(level of "game process" and rules comprehension)*

0	1	2	3	4
very low	low	moderate	high	very high
(misses the point)	(rigid)	(grasps the process)	(teaches others)	(invents new ways to play)

WINNING *(level of concern to win or succeed)*

0	1	2	3	4
very low	low	moderate	high	very high
(could care less)	(maybe next time)	(frustrated by loss)	(desire to improve)	(winning is everything)

STRATEGY *(level of skill and game execution)*

0	1	2	3	4
very low	low	moderate	high	very high
(no desire to learn)	(makes big mistakes)	(frustrated by loss)	(has a strategy)	(adapts strategy)

ATTENTION *(level of awareness and interest)*

0	1	2	3	4
very low	low	moderate	high	very high
(bored)	(easily distracted)	(curious)	(deeply involved)	(focused concentration)

Intelligence Skill Games Scoring

(adapted from the Gloucester Spectrum Project)

2. For each intelligence area, total the numbers from the observation chart and divide by 7. Record these numbers on the following table:

Verbal-Linguistic Games	Logical-Mathematical Games	Visual-Spatial Games	Bodily-Kinesthetic Games	Musical-Rhythmic Games	Interpersonal Games	Intrapersonal Games

3. Turn to the Multiple Intelligences Profile Indicator on page 71 and graph the score by darkening the appropriate segment(s) for each intelligence area.

NOTES AND REFLECTIONS

Multiple Intelligence Approaches to Assessment © 1994 Zephyr Press, Tucson, Arizona

Intelligence Foci

 ## Procedure

Show students a film, play, or TV show that includes fine representations of the intelligences—beautiful scenery, great soundtrack, lots of action, good script, and so on. Afterward, lead students in a discussion, carefully listening to what they focused their attention on, what captured their imagination, and what they liked or disliked.

Intelligence Foci

Student Name: _____ Age: ____ Date of Observation: _____

Verbal-Linguistic Discussion Questions 0 1 2 3 4

What lines of dialogue do you remember?
What were some of the key words, phrases, or figures of speech used?
What written words do you remember from any of the scenes?

Logical-Mathematical Discussion Questions 0 1 2 3 4

Where were you aware of the use or presence of patterns?
What do you think would happen in a sequel to what you have seen?
How would you compare and contrast the major characters?

Visual-Spatial Discussion Questions 0 1 2 3 4

What scenes do you remember?
What physical objects do you remember? What colors? What visual patterns?
What symbols were used?

Bodily-Kinesthetic Discussion Questions 0 1 2 3 4

What action scenes can you recall?
What gestures and physical movements did the main characters use?
Where were you aware of movement of any kind?

Musical-Rhythmic Discussion Questions 0 1 2 3 4

What sounds and noises do you remember?
Where were you aware of music being used? Can you hum any of the themes?
What sounds or music would you add to the production if you could?

Interpersonal Discussion Questions 0 1 2 3 4

What are your observations about how the various characters related?
If you could have one of the characters as a friend, who would you choose? Why?
What role would you assign each main character on a team or in a cooperative group?

Intrapersonal Discussion Questions 0 1 2 3 4

Where were you aware of your own emotions and feelings?
With whom did you identify? Whom did you dislike and why?
In a sentence, state what you think the message or moral is.
   What title would you give the film?

Intelligence Foci Scoring

Instructions

1. During the discussion, try to detect the different intelligences students used when watching the same movie, play, or TV show. Listen for clues such as those listed below, which reveal different ways in which students are processing the production. Rank the students based on the frequency and intensity of their comments using the following criteria:

> **0** = unable to recall information related to the questions; is bored by these kinds of questions
>
> **1** = recalls mostly items already mentioned by others; shows little interest in these questions
>
> **2** = remembers new things that piggyback on or are related to others' responses; shows some interest in answering these questions but loses interest quickly
>
> **3** = recalls new items from contexts and situations not mentioned previously; demonstrates an appreciation for subtleties of things in the area; interprets the meaning of specific items; items from the discussion of one intelligence trigger responses from another intelligence
>
> **4** = keeps coming back to items from this area; shows genuine appreciation for and excitement about questions related to this area; based on information from this area, is able to hypothesize, empathize, analyze, and perform higher-order cognitive tasks related to the larger story; sees connections between items and questions in this area and everyday living

Clues for Listening between the Lines of the Discussion

(What to be looking for)

VERBAL-LINGUISTIC

- remembers specific phrases and patterns of speech
- interprets characters primarily through their speech
- easily recalls written and verbal information from the production
- appreciates linguistically based humor

LOGICAL-MATHEMATICAL

- grasps thought and behavior patterns of various characters
- tries to figure out what is going to happen next based on clues
- analyzes cause-and-effect relationships
- notices and points out various motifs in the story

Intelligence Foci Scoring (continued)

VISUAL-SPATIAL

- recalls details of the physical setting and scenery
- expresses an awareness of colors, objects, textures, visual symbols, and patterns
- is able to imagine alternatives to what actually happened
- can pretend or fantasize based on the production

BODILY-KINESTHETIC

- is sensitive to the body language and gestures of the characters
- is preoccupied or fascinated with the action scenes
- is able to recall what characters were doing in various scenes
- is aware of own physical responses to what was happening on the screen or stage

MUSICAL-RHYTHMIC

- is aware of the use of music to enhance various scenes
- is sensitive to a variety of sounds and noises
- understands characters through the tone, pitch, inflection, or rhythm of their speech
- is aware of the pacing and rhythm of the production

INTERPERSONAL

- expresses empathy with various characters
- analyzes positive and negative relating patterns of the characters
- is concerned with the human factor in the story
- is able to understand and defend varied points of view in the story

INTRAPERSONAL

- is aware of own feelings while watching the production
- exhibits identification with various characters
- is conscious of values, beliefs, and ethical implications of the production
- expresses new self-understanding and raises personal questions

Intelligence Foci Scoring (continued)

2. Record the intelligence attention foci scores on the table below.

Verbal-Linguistic	Logical-Mathematical	Visual-Spatial	Bodily-Kinesthetic	Musical-Rhythmic	Interpersonal	Intrapersonal

3. Turn to the Multiple Intelligences Profile Indicator on page 71 and graph these scores by darkening the appropriate segment(s) for each intelligence area.

NOTES AND REFLECTIONS

Complex Problem Solving

 ## Procedure

Expose students to a variety of problem-solving tasks that will potentially stimulate several intelligences in the students' efforts to find a solution. Make sure students know they can do anything to find an answer, regardless of how the problem is framed. Then watch what they do and the strategies they try.

Complex Problem Solving

⭐ **Student Name:** _____ **Age:** _____

Date of Observation: _____

SCENARIO 1

A man and a woman are walking down the street together. They want to stay together, but the woman's stride is two-thirds the length of the man's. They both start out with their left feet. How many steps will they each have to take until they step on their left feet at the same time again?

SCENARIO 2

The city has decided to create a new playground. They want your students to give them ideas about what it should look like. Ask your students to think about things they would like to be part of the new playground as well as what they imagine it would look like. Have them prepare a presentation to help the city council understand their ideas.

SCENARIO 3

Create a problem based on human traffic patterns in the school and ask students to come up with solutions. You may build the problem around cafeteria lines, congestion in the halls when school lets out each day, congestion going to and from school assemblies, fire drill procedures, and so on.

SCENARIO 4

Create a problem based on the reduction of noise pollution in your school, various neighborhoods in the community, or in a home. Ask students to analyze the issue as well as to find solutions they think would work.

SCENARIO 5

Create a problem based on human relationships, such as a misunderstanding, a broken promise, a breakdown in communication, some type of prejudice, a disagreement between two people, and so on. Ask students to look for a number of solutions to the problem.

Complex Problem Solving Scoring

Instructions

1. Carefully observe students involved in the act of trying to solve the problems you have presented. Watch for the use of various problem-solving strategies that reflect the different intelligences.

Use the strategy checklists below to guide your observations. Feel free to add other strategies you observe.

Intelligence-Specific Problem-Solving Strategy Checklists

VERBAL-LINGUISTIC

- linguistic analysis and clarification of the problem
- persuasive speaking or verbal debate
- information search through reading or asking questions
- definition of terms of the problem
- written report of solutions
- _____

LOGICAL-MATHEMATICAL

- inductive or deductive thinking
- numerical patterns or equations
- math processes or operations
- calculation or measurement
- logical rationales for solutions
- _____

Complex Problem Solving Scoring *(continued)*

VISUAL-SPATIAL
- diagrams, pictures, designs, and symbols
- visualization or imagination
- maps, blueprints, or flowcharts
- manipulatives
- colors and textures
- _____

BODILY-KINESTHIC
- dance/physical exercise movements
- dramatization
- physical gestures
- creating models or inventing
- physical simulation
- _____

MUSICAL-RHYTHMIC
- environmental sounds
- singing or humming
- composition
- tonal or rhythmic patterns
- recognition of auditory schemas
- _____

INTERPERSONAL
- discussion of solutions
- piggybacking ideas
- consensus building and compromise
- teamwork and division of labor
- positive and negative aspects of various solutions
- _____

INTRAPERSONAL
- solitary reflection or thinking
- affective processing or analysis
- focused concentration
- metacognitive processing or thinking
- self-identity posturing
- _____

Multiple Intelligence Approaches to Assessment © 1994 Zephyr Press, Tucson, Arizona

Complex Problem Solving Scoring (continued)

2. Record on the table below the number of distinct strategies from each intelligence area you see students use.
    Note: If a score is greater than 4, record it as a 4+.

Verbal-Linguistic	Logical-Mathematical	Visual-Spatial	Bodily-Kinesthetic	Musical-Rhythmic	Interpersonal	Intrapersonal

3. Turn to the Multiple Intelligences Profile Indicator on page 71 and graph these scores by darkening the appropriate segments for each intelligence area.

NOTES AND REFLECTIONS

Inventing

 ## Procedure

Provide students with an opportunity to design or create a project. Set up stations or labs around the room that have the tools of the different intelligences as well as project ideas. Give students time to create, watching to see **which labs they are drawn to** *as well as* **what they do once they begin to create.**

Inventing

Student Name: _____ **Age:** _____ **Date of Observation:** _____

Project Media and Ideas

Verbal-Linguistic

The station should include paper, pencils, pens, dictionaries, thesaurus, tape recorder, typewriter or word processor, poetry books, joke books, magazines, and other written materials.

PROJECT IDEAS ● ● ● ● ● ● ● ● ● ● ● ● ● ●

- ★ Writing essays or reports
- ★ Writing poetry and limericks
- ★ Defining key vocabulary words
- ★ Formal speaking (persuasive or explanatory)
- ★ Debate

Visual-Spatial

The station should include paints, colored markers, clay, videos, colored construction paper, building blocks, Legos™, maps, posters, books and magazines with a lot of pictures, scissors, and paste.

PROJECT IDEAS ● ● ● ● ● ● ● ● ● ● ● ● ● ●

- ★ Creating graphic illustrations (pictures and murals)
- ★ Making sculptures (clay and dirt)
- ★ Creating montages and collages
- ★ Making flowcharts
- ★ Designing posters and brochures

Logical-Mathematical

The station should include calculators, computers, rulers, and books containing graphic organizers.

PROJECT IDEAS ● ● ● ● ● ● ● ● ● ● ● ● ●

- ★ Creating annotated outlines
- ★ Reporting statistics
- ★ Demonstrating thinking patterns such as comparison/contrast
- ★ Explaining the steps involved in a process

Bodily-Kinesthetic

The station should include costumes, makeup, sports equipment, and material for building or inventing something.

PROJECT IDEAS ● ● ● ● ● ● ● ● ● ● ● ● ●

- ★ Creating a drama, role-play, or mime
- ★ Dancing (both traditional and creative or original)
- ★ Creating human tableaux
- ★ Creating physical routines (body language, gestures, exercise)
- ★ Building something

Inventing

Project Media and Ideas (continued)

Musical-Rhythmic

The station should include musical instruments, percussion instruments, audiocassette players, a variety of music and sound tapes, and various kinds of noisemakers.

PROJECT IDEAS • • • • • • • • • • • • • • • •

★ Creating a musical TV ad or jingle
★ Creating a sound accompaniment on tape
★ Writing songs (original or known tunes)
★ Exploring rhythmic and beat factors (cultures, seasons, body processes)

Intrapersonal

This station should include solitary, quiet space to walk; blank paper for journal entries, sets of journal writing "starters" (see *Seven Pathways of Learning*), a list of self-reflective questions to consider

PROJECT IDEAS • • • • • • • • • • • • • •

★ Writing autobiographies
★ Writing or drawing in personal, reflective journals
★ Doing thinking logs
★ Keeping self-understanding diaries

Interpersonal

This station should include lists of things to do with a partner, group projects, things to talk about, and suggestions for working together

PROJECT IDEAS • • • • • • • • • • • • • •

★ Doing think-pair-share (see *7 Pathways of Learning*)
★ Putting together a jigsaw project with a team
★ Doing each one teach one (see *7 Pathways of Learning*)
★ Competing on teams
★ Taking questionnaires and surveys

Inventing Scoring

Project Observation and Analysis Sheet

Instructions

1. Place a check mark by each of the following items you observe in students' inventions or projects. Feel free to add other items to the checklists.

Verbal-Linguistic

___ use of humor
___ definition of terms (vocabulary)
___ carefully written report or explanations
___ persuasive speeches or defenses of ideas
___ other

Logical-Mathematical

___ statistical reporting or analysis
___ noticing various patterns
___ use of cognitive or graphic organizers
___ logical thinking or analysis
___ other

Visual-Spatial

___ use of visual aids (images and so on)
___ colorful or "textureful" product
___ project that provokes imagination
___ project is visually pleasing or stimulating (neat, balanced, and so on)
___ other

Bodily-Kinesthetic

___ hands-on or experiential project (learning by doing)
___ report involves demonstration
___ project shows nonbook research (field trip, experiments, and so on)
___ other

Musical-Rhythmic

___ project has audio components beyond talking
___ use of different tonal patterns
___ use of different rhythms and beats
___ incorporation of some kind of music
___ other

Interpersonal

___ project is team effort
___ project involves person-to-person interaction and communication
___ use of questionnaires and surveys
___ encourages questions and input from others
___ other

Intrapersonal

___ explains feelings about project
___ project shows implications and applications
___ exhibits evidence of higher-order thinking
___ evidence of integration with other subject areas and beyond school
___ other

Inventing Scoring *(continued)*

2. Tally the number of check marks per intelligence and record the results on the following table:

Verbal-Linguistic Components	Logical-Mathematical Components	Visual-Spatial Components	Bodily-Kinesthetic Components	Musical-Rhythmic Components	Interpersonal Components	Intrapersonal Components

3. Turn to the Multiple Intelligences Profile Indicator on page 71 and graph these scores by darkening the appropriate segment(s) for each intelligence area.

NOTES AND REFLECTIONS

Multiple Intelligences Profile Indicator

Instrument Key
BL = Behavior Log
SG = Skill Games
IF = Intelligence Foci
CP = Complex Problems
I = Inventing

Scoring Key
0 = no interest
1 = low interest
2 = definite interest
3 = high interest
4 = extraordinary interest

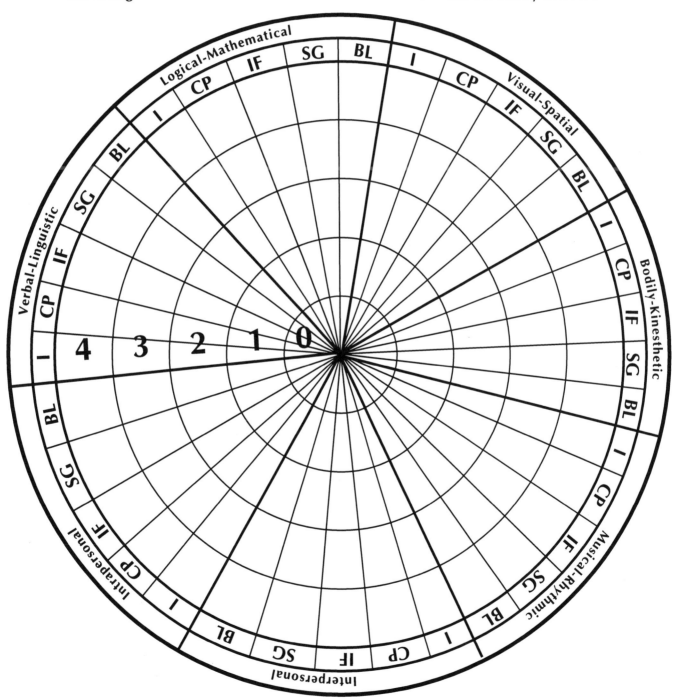

4

Prescriptions for Expanding and Enhancing Intelligence

Using Intelligence Profiles to Help Students

Once we have intelligence profiles for our students we have initial pictures of what makes student tick intellectually. These profiles also provide us with new knowledge about how to help all students (regardless of their relative strengths and weaknesses in the various intelligence areas) get more out of school. Following is a description and interpretation of varying profile dominances for each intelligence area. I have also expanded on and updated the Multiple Intelligences Toolbox from *Seven Ways of Knowing*. The new toolbox includes a set of easily integrated strategies and ideas for moving lessons to multiple levels. In integrating the strategies, I believe that we will begin reaching students who have intelligence profiles very different from the verbal-linguistic and logical-mathematical profiles.

Verbal-Linguistic Profile Dominance

 These students have highly developed verbal skills and often think in words. They like reading, playing word games, making up poetry and stories, getting into involved discussions, debating, formal speaking, creative writing, and telling jokes. They tend to be precise in expressing themselves, they love learning new words, they do well on written assignments, and their comprehension of what they have read is high.

You can help these students by encouraging them to develop fully and refine their verbal-linguistic abilities. To reach and teach them effectively, design lessons that incorporate the following tools:

Reading—study various written materials on a subject, for example, library research projects

Vocabulary—learn new word meanings and practice using them accurately in regular communication

Formal speaking—make verbal presentations to others

Journal/Diary keeping—trace and keep track of own thoughts and ideas

Creative writing—write original works with no boundaries

Poetry—create own poetic expression and reading; appreciate other people's poetry

Debate—present both sides of an issue in a convincing manner

Impromptu speaking—speak instantly on a random topic

Humor/Jokes—create puns, limericks, and jokes on academic topics

Storytelling/Story creation—make up or tell stories about anything being studied

Logical-Mathematical Profile Dominance

 These students think conceptually and abstractly and are able to see patterns and relationships that others often miss. They like to experiment, solve puzzles and other problems, ask cosmic questions, and think. They generally enjoy working with numbers and mathematical formulas and operations. They love the challenge of a complex problem to solve. They tend to be systematic and analytical, and they always have a logical rationale or argument for what they are doing or thinking.

You can help these students by encouraging them to develop fully and use their logical thought processes. To reach and teach them effectively, design lessons that incorporate the following tools:

Abstract symbols and formulas—design meaningful summary notation systems for a variety of processes or knowledge content

Outlining—invent point-by-point logical explanations for items

Graphic/Cognitive organizers—work with logical thought maps such as webs, Venn diagrams, classification matrices, and so on

Number sequences/patterns—investigate numerical facts (for example, statistics of graphs) about a topic

Calculation—use specified steps and operations to solve a problem (for example, story problems or putting together clues to solve a mystery)

Deciphering codes—work to understand and communicate using various kinds of symbolic language

Forcing relationships—put noncongruent ideas together and create meaningful connections among them

Syllogisms—make closed logical "if . . . then . . . " deductions about a topic

Problem solving—list appropriate procedures for varied problem-solving situations

Logic/Pattern games—create puzzles that challenge others to find a hidden rationale or pattern

Visual-Spatial Profile Dominance

 These students think in images and pictures. They are often very aware of objects, shapes, colors, and patterns in their environment. They like to draw, paint, make interesting designs and patterns, and work with clay, colored construction paper, and fabric. They love jigsaw puzzles, reading maps and finding their way around new places, and daydreaming. They have strong opinions about such things as colors that go together, textures that are appropriate and pleasing, and decorating. They are excellent at performing tasks that require seeing with the mind's eye (for example, visualizing, pretending, imagining, and forming mental images).

You can help these students by frequently asking them to express themselves and their thoughts through pictures, images, symbols, colors, designs, and patterns. To reach and teach them effectively, design lessons that incorporate the following tools:

Visualizing—create pictures and images of items in the mind (for example, characters in a story, a period of history, a scientific process)

Active imagination—associate or find connections between visual designs and patterns and prior experiences and knowledge

Color/Texture schemes—associate colors and textures with various thoughts, ideas, concepts, and processes

Patterns/Designs—create abstract patterns and designs to represent the dynamics of and relationships among different pieces of knowledge

Painting—express understanding of concepts using the medium of paints or colored markers (for example, mural creation)

Drawing—create graphic representations of items being studied (for example, diagrams, illustrations, flowcharts, and so on)

Sculpting—demonstrate understanding of concepts by creating models in clay

Mind mapping—create "webs" that use images, shapes, patterns, colors, designs, and pictures of written information or concepts

Pretending/Fantasy—create interesting scenarios in the mind based on factual information

Montage/Collage—design a collection of pictures and/or fabric, natural objects (shells, leaves, sand, etc.), or uncooked macaroni to show various aspects or dimensions of a concept, idea, or process

Multiple Intelligence Approaches to Assessment © 1994 Zephyr Press, Tucson, Arizona

Bodily-Kinesthetic Profile Dominance

 These students have a keen sense of body awareness. They like physical movement, hugging, dancing, making and inventing things with their hands, and role-playing. They communicate well through body language and other physical gestures. They can often perform a task only after seeing someone else do it first and then mimicking the actions. They generally like physical games of all kinds and demonstrating how to do something. They find it difficult to sit still for a long time and are easily bored if they are not actively involved in what is going on around them.

You can help these students by giving them hands-on activities and frequent opportunities to get their bodies into their learning. To reach and teach them effectively, design lessons that incorporate the following tools:

Folk dance/Creative dance—choreograph a dance that demonstrates something learned

Role-playing/Mime—show understanding of concepts and ideas through such things as skits and charades

Dramatic enactment—create a mini-drama that shows the dynamic interplay of various factors, processes, or ideas

Physical exercise/Martial arts—teach others something by creating physical routines to be performed

Body language/Physical gestures—embody meaning, interpretation, or understanding of something in physical movement

Inventing—make or build something to demonstrate a concept, idea, or process (for example, a model to show how something works)

Sports games—create a contest or game based on specific knowledge about a given subject being studied

Gymnastic routines—design an orchestrated flow of physical movement that embodies relationships and connections within a topic being studied

Human graph—stand along a continuum to express agreement or understanding of a concept, idea, or process

Body sculpture/Tableaux—arrange or sculpt a group to express an idea, concept, or process

Musical-Rhythmic Profile Dominance

 These students love music and rhythmic patterns. They are very sensitive to sounds in the environment: the chirp of a cricket, rain on the roof, varying traffic patterns. They may study better with music in the background. They can often reproduce a melody or rhythmic pattern after hearing it only once. Various sounds, tones, and rhythms may have a visible effect on them (that is, you can see a change in facial expressions, body movement, or emotional responses). They like to create music. They enjoy singing and listening to a wide variety of music. They are often quite skilled at mimicking sounds, language accents, and others' speech patterns, and recognizing different musical instruments in a composition.

You can help these students by encouraging them to explore the sound, music, and rhythm dimensions of lessons. To reach and teach them effectively, design lessons that incorporate the following tools:

Rhythmic patterns/Percussion vibrations—illustrate an academic concept by producing rhythms, beats, and vibrational patterns to show its various aspects

Vocal sounds/Tones—illustrate something being studied with sounds produced by the vocal chords

Music composition and creation—compose or create music to communicate understanding of a concept, idea, or process (for example, the stages of a cell dividing)

Rapping—use raps to help communicate or remember certain concepts, ideas, or processes

Environmental sounds—use the natural sounds that are part of something being studied and learned (for example, weather conditions, geographical situations, animals)

Instrumental sounds—use musical instruments to produce sounds for a lesson (for example, background accompaniment, enhancements for teaching)

Singing/Humming—create songs and/or vocal chord sounds about various pieces of academic content

Tonal patterns—recognize the tone dimension of topics being studied (for example, the sounds a computer makes, weather conditions, sounds of animals)

Musical performance—present a report in which music and rhythm play a central role

Musical/Rhythmic "schemas"—find existing songs, instrumental or musical themes, or various kinds of rhythmic beats that go with what is being studied

Interpersonal Profile Dominance

 These students learn through person-to-person inter-action. They generally have lots of friends, show a great deal of empathy for other people and understanding of different points of view. They love team activities of all kinds and are very good team members, pulling their own weight and often much more. They are sensitive to other people's feelings and ideas, are good at piggybacking their ideas on others' thoughts, and are skilled at drawing others out in a discussion. They are also often very skilled in conflict resolution and mediation when people are in radical opposition to each other.

You can help these students by using high-challenge, cooperative learning situations in the classroom. To reach and teach them effectively, design lessons that incorporate the following tools:

Giving feedback—offer honest, sensitive input on one's performance and expressed opinions

Intuiting others' feelings—second-guess what someone else is feeling or experiencing in a given situation

Cooperative learning strategies—structure teamwork in the academic learning situation

Person-to-person communication—focus on the ways people relate and how to improve their relating

Empathy practices—express understanding from someone else's viewpoint or life experience

Jigsaw—divide the learning and teaching of a topic into distinct segments and assign students to learn from and teach each other

Collaborative skills teaching—focus on learning and recognition of the social skills needed for effective person-to-person relating

Receiving feedback—accept another's input or reaction to own performance and opinions

Sensing others' motivations—explore a topic through others' motivations in certain situations or explore why others made certain decisions

Group projects—assign students to investigate or study a topic with others in a team

Intrapersonal Profile Dominance

 These students like to work alone and sometimes shy away from others. They are self-reflective and self-aware and thus tend to be in tune with their inner feelings, values, beliefs, and thinking processes. They are frequently bearers of creative wisdom and insight, are highly intuitive, and are inwardly motivated rather than needing external rewards to keep them going. They are often strong willed, self-confident, and have definite, well-thought out opinions on almost any issue (albeit they are sometimes a little "off the wall"). Other students will often come to them for advice and counsel, but other students will also sometimes view them as distant and weird.

You can help these students by frequently asking them to "go inside" and be aware of their feelings, thought processes, and reflections, and by giving them independent study assignments. To reach and teach them effectively, design lessons that incorporate the following tools:

Silent reflection methods—have students work with such things as reflective journals, thinking logs, and learning diaries

Metacognitive techniques—use techniques that promote thinking about one's thinking (that is, tracing the various processes and steps used in a topic of study)

Thinking strategies planning—have students consciously decide the thinking patterns and processes to use for a given task

Emotional processing—be aware of the affective dimensions (that is, "How does it make me feel?") of something being studied

"Know thyself"/Introspective procedures—state personal implications, applications, and self-discovery insights of classroom learning in personal life

Mindfulness practices—use techniques that foster paying attention to one's own life experience (the opposite of mindlessness or "living on automatic pilot")

Focusing/Concentration skills—bring the mind to a single point of focus and hold it there to complete a task

Higher-order reasoning—move thinking from memorization of facts to understanding of process to a grasp of synthesis, integration, and application of learning

"Altered states of consciousness" practices—know how to shift moods and awareness to optimal states

Independent studies and projects—give "work-alone" assignments in which students express feelings, thoughts, implications, and their personal philosophy on a topic

Strength or Weakness: Where Should We Focus?

In professional development workshops, teachers often ask me, "Should we teach to students' strengths or focus on developing their weaknesses?" My answer is always "YES!" I believe we should be doing both. The importance of creating intelligence profiles (chapter 3) and the prescriptive strategies presented in this chapter is that they give us ways to emphasize and highlight students' strengths while helping us find ways to work on developing the weaker intelligences.

In my own teaching I have found that it is generally best to use a stronger, more developed, more "comfortable" intelligence to help students when they are learning something new or when they are trying to grasp or understand a particularly difficult concept. Sometimes, *if given the chance,* students will also ask to be tested using an intelligence with which they feel more comfortable, for they feel more confident of success.

I usually like to ask students to stretch and use other intelligences that are not as strong when I want them to do creative or higher-order thinking about something they are studying, when I want them to make applications beyond what is presented in the textbook or classroom lecture, when I want to help them see connections between what they have been studying and other aspects of the curriculum and their life beyond school, and when I want to check for genuine understanding of the material. Using a weaker intelligence can also often help students understand difficult concepts—if they can't get it in one way, often approaching it through another doorway will help them understand.

It is also possible to use a stronger intelligence to "train" or empower a weaker intelligence. One of the mistakes we often make in the various remedial programs that we create to help children with their schooling is that we remediate at the point of their weakness; for example, the prescription for children who are not good readers and really don't like reading is often to spend more time doing precisely what they are not very good at and what they don't like. Doing this is somewhat akin to prescribing louder speaking to communicate with someone who is totally deaf! In the case of so-called nonreaders, I have found it produces far greater success to watch them carefully to determine what they are good at and what they love doing. Once I know this, it is possible to lead them through the doorway of their strength and what they really enjoy, and work on the reading from that perspective.

Following are several examples of using a strength in one intelligence to train, enhance, and develop a weaker intelligence. These examples are just a few of hundreds I could give from teachers who have incorporated a multiple intelligence approach in their daily instruction.

Teaching for a Musical-Rhythmic Dominance

A high school science teacher in the Chicago area told me about a student in his freshman honors biology class who had high achievement scores but was totally lost studying genetics. The teacher also knew that the student was very skilled at music composition. This teacher hit upon the idea of using music to help the student grasp the genetic code. Sometimes the genetic code is varied by what is called a "frame shift" (the first base of a three-based code is skipped). The teacher asked the student to take a song the student had composed (one that was in three-quarter time) and drop off the first note of the song. The student was then to rewrite the song by simply(?!) moving each note up one space. He understood immediately and saw that the process creates a totally new song. To illustrate inversion the teacher had the student write and play the song backward. For deletion (a three-base code is omitted), the teacher had the student take any bar out of the song and notice that a different melody results. In this case, the student was able to make the transfer of learning to genetics by coming through the doorway of his highly developed musical-rhythmic intelligence.

Teaching for a Bodily-Kinesthetic Dominance

A second grade teacher in El Paso, Texas, shared a "kinesthetic spelling" lesson she designed to help some of her students who were having a great deal of difficulty remembering how to spell words correctly when it came to a test or their daily writing. She noticed, however, these same students had no trouble at all remembering the fairly complex rules and physical movments involved in a wide variety of playground games. She decided to tap into this "body knowing" by teaching these students how to spell with their bodies. Basically, the children were to make their bodies into the shapes of the different letters of a word. For example, students would make a "Y" by standing straight and extending the arms over the head in an outstretched fashion; they would make a "B" by placing the left hand on the hip and raising the left foot and leg to the calf of the right leg; and so on. The teacher told me that since she figured out how to put spelling into the language of body movement, these children have consistently scored better than 85 percent on spelling tests!

Teaching for a Visual-Spatial Dominance

A middle school teacher in Rochester, New York, had a number of students in her class who were having difficulty with reading comprehension, but she knew from the art teacher (as well as her own "profile observations") that these students loved to draw and paint and were doing very well in art class. She decided to see if she could help them develop greater reading comprehension by coming at it through a visual-spatial doorway. She first of all worked with the students by reading something to them and having them draw what she was reading, for example, a scene, characters, some action, people relating, and so on. She then asked the students to explain their drawings. The teacher worked with them to make sure they had images, patterns, designs, and so on, that told the full story she had read.

She then had the students tell the story, based on their drawings, into a tape recorder. Next they listened to the recording and wrote it on paper. Finally, they read the story they had written from the tape to other students, using their pictures to enhance the story. The teacher told me she has seen a marked improvement in her students' comprehension capacities as a result of this approach.

I believe that *anything* we have to teach can be taught in ways that incorporate all seven intelligences. We must first of all, however, take the time to translate it into the symbol sytems, language, jargon, and vernacular of the various intelligences, as in the examples presented earlier. Second, we must help students understand themselves intellectually: they must understand that they do indeed possess multiple ways of being smart; that there are many ways to learn something and to process information; and that practicing and consciously using the different intelligences can enhance, strengthen, and expand the intelligences. Third, we need to work in a very systematic way to integrate the teaching of the full spectrum of intelligence capacities in and through the curriculum in ways that are developmentally appropriate. What this would mean is that year by year, as students move through our systems of formal education, we continually help them expand their repertoire of intelligence capabilities so that, instead of there being fewer and fewer opportunities to express themselves and their learning through art, drama, music, and dance, for example, every year we teach them increasingly complex and higher-order ways to use and appreciate at least all seven intelligences. In doing so, I believe we will help our students reach their full intellectual potential.

5

Assessing Student Academic Progress

Toward Creating Authentic Assessments

(Theoretical Background)

It seems that we have forgotten something very important in our Western systems of education when it comes to evaluating students' academic progress; namely, assessment should be an opportunity to enhance, empower, and celebrate students' learning. Instead, we too often use it as an opportunity to point out students' failures. This is one of the faces of the deficit-based approach to assessment (discussed in chapter 2). I know of few adults who would put up with what we expect students to deal with for at least twelve years; namely, being in a situation where day in and day out, year after year, they are being told, multiple times and in many ways, where and how they are failing. Then we are surprised that many students experience problems with self-esteem!

The second face of the deficit-based approach manifests itself in the almost compulsive need we as a society have to rank students in terms of their supposed academic ability, to compare them to one another, and to determine the quality of our schools based on students' standardized test scores, which we compare by publishing them in the newspaper. Rarely, if ever, do we question the test scores' validity or what they really tell us. Thomas Armstrong makes the following point in *In Their Own Way*: "Tests are supposed to give parents and teachers information about how children are progressing in their learning. Instead, *they tend to reduce children and all of their thoughts, feelings, behaviors, and achievements to a handful of percentiles, rankings, letter grades, and fancy-sounding labels*" (32; emphasis mine).

In a staff development workshop I was conducting once, we got involved in a fairly lively discussion about how we approach assessment of student academic progress in our schools. I was making a number of observations similar to those here, suggesting that we need to turn the tables and use assessment as a grand opportunity to celebrate students' achievements, their success, the new knowledge they have gained, and the personal growth they have experienced. One teacher finally interrupted me and said, "But if I did what you are suggesting, all of my students could get A's. Then what would I do? How would I explain this to my principal?"

In response to the first question, I suggested, "Have a grand party!" And in response to the question about the principal, "Invite her or him to the party!"

In this interchange we see another face of the assessment conundrum. We assume that not all students can (*or should*) be successful in school. Nowhere is this assumption more evident than in standardized testing. Standardized modes of testing made their way into American education during the heyday of the industrial revolution. At that time, the nation was seeking efficient ways to do everything. We were looking for anything that would streamline, standardize, mechanize, and generally accelerate the production of all goods and services. What this meant in industry was assembly lines. We thought that this same "mechanistic paradigm" could be applied to human beings.

We are only now beginning to reap the harvest of what was sown. We have created a situation in which the need of students to be assessed authentically and thoroughly and the need of teachers for time to reflect deeply about fair test designs and effective grading practices are being made subordinate to the cost-saving policies of budget makers, to the arbitrary dictates of college admissions officers, to bottom-line-oriented employers, and to the efficiency-driven needs of secretaries who enter grades into computers. Authentic assessment is not, and never will be, efficient. Authentic assessment is effective, however, in helping students learn and in promoting high standards in our schools.

One of the underlying suppositions that we must change if we are to be aligned with the new assessment paradigm (to say nothing of the findings of current educational research) is that the evaluation of learning and knowledge happens on a bell-shaped curve. In fact this model precludes all students

Multiple Intelligence Approaches to Assessment © 1994 Zephyr Press, Tucson, Arizona

succeeding, for some MUST fail, MOST are average, and only a FEW can be truly successful. Grant Wiggins (1988) makes the following observation about such assessment:

> The harmful effects of norm-referenced testing on students are both moral and intellectual. The "bell curve" is an intended result in test design, not some coincidental statistical result of mass testing—a design feature that assumes teachers have no or only random effect on students. The "norm" of the curve, being a merely comparative statistic and unrelated to any intellectual standard, does not obligate the test-maker to insure that the test assesses the kind of work that matters most. . . .
>
> Current standardized tests and their scoring systems thus serve everyone but teachers and students. They are deliberately designed to yield maximal differences in single scores for purposes of quick ranking, sorting, and comparing of cross-school groups, often exaggerating the actual range of student achievement. And by now we know how absurd the "norms" used to design the tests really are, when every state, like every student of Lake Wobegone, is "above average." (2 of reprint)

In addition to these difficulties, typical tests tend to produce students who have figured out how to "play the game of school," and thus graduate, but who are inadequately equipped to deal with the realities of post-modern living. The subtext of current standardized testing practices is, "If you get the right answers, who cares if you really know and understand the material?" Education is thus reduced to teaching students simply how to jump through a prescribed set of hoops created outside of the daily learning and teaching environment, much like what is involved in training a performing circus animal.

In a staff development workshop I was conducting, I had just made the point about standardized tests and circus animals when I was suddenly interrupted by a teacher who said, "Yes, but even circus animals are taught to perform 'in context.' Our standardized tests are so far from the real world and require such low-level thinking and understanding that they are hard to take seriously from any genuine academic or reflective intellectual standpoint!"

Essentially, the bell-shaped curve, often used in one form or another to evaluate students, sorts them into general achievement categories based on students' performance on various kinds of norm-referenced examinations (see diagram that follows). We must not delude ourselves as we interpret what this sorting reveals. It may in fact tell us little about the knowledge students have actually gained or what they have learned and understand in a given area of academic pursuit. It probably does give us, however, a fairly accurate picture that about 10 percent of our students do very well on these kinds of tests, 10 percent do poorly, and about 80 percent fall in the middle, or average, range!

The bell-shaped curve does have its uses, however. It is an excellent tool for sorting people into various categories such as likes and dislikes of certain topics, shoe size, hair color, age, weight, and TV viewing preferences. This kind

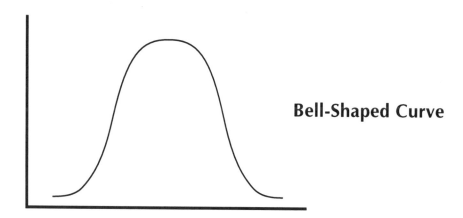

Bell-Shaped Curve

of information does indeed tend to fall along a bell-shaped curve. It is also valuable for finding an average given certain variables or categories. Unfortunately (or fortunately, depending on your perspective), however, the growth of human knowledge does not occur along a bell-shaped curve. It is simply not an accurate picture of how knowing, understanding, and learning happen!

J-Curve

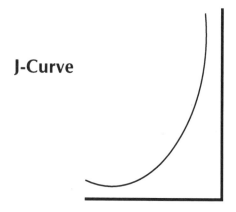

The J-curve is a far more accurate picture of the growth of knowledge (see diagram). This curve suggests that knowledge grows in a compounding fashion. We start with a little knowledge and then, year by year, we build on this knowledge so that our foundation of knowing is enhanced, expanded, and deepened as we mature. If our assessment practices are to reflect this growth, we must provide opportunities for students to demonstrate their growing knowledge and learning to us in whatever ways they can. Students must be assisted to know what they know fully. What this means is that assessment should genuinely benefit students. Howard Gardner (1993) says,

In my own view, psychologists spend far too much time ranking individuals and not nearly enough time helping them. Assessment should be undertaken primarily to aid students. It is incumbent upon the assessor to provide feedback to the student that will be helpful at the present time—identifying areas of strength as well as weakness, giving suggestions of what to study or work on, pointing out what habits are productive and which are not, indicating what can be expected in the way of future assessment, and the like. It is especially important that some of the feedback take the form of concrete suggestions and indicate relative strengths to build upon, independent of rank within a comparative group of students. (178)

Students must also have a chance to make connections between what happens in the classroom and other areas or aspects of the particular discipline being studied, other subject areas of the academic curriculum (both formal and informal), and life in the so-called real world. What this means is that any assessment should be a direct teaching and learning experience that focuses on the transfer, integration, synthesis, and application of one's learning.

I am not opposed to standardized tests per se, nor to traditional paper-and-pencil examinations. I am opposed, however, to allowing these assessment instruments to tell the whole story about our students. We must recognize that they tell an important *part* of the story, *but only a part!* Grant Wiggins (1989) makes the following important point:

> A genuine test of intellectual achievement doesn't merely check 'standardized' work in a mechanical way. It reveals achievement on the essentials, even if they are not easily quantified. . . . Standardized tests have no more effect on a student's intellectual health than taking a pulse has on a patient's physical health. If we want standardized tests to be authentic, to help students learn about themselves and about the subject matter or field being tested, they must become more than merely indicators of one superficial symptom. (704)

We must devise and use other means of assessment that paint a whole picture of students' learning. Of necessity, these new approaches will go beyond (but include) traditional standardized and paper-and-pencil tests.

In the same article, Wiggins discusses some of the moral issues involved in standardized approaches to testing:

> The standardized test is disrespectful by design. Mass testing as we know it treats students as objects—as if their education and thought processes were similar and as if the reasons for their answers were irrelevant. Test-takers are not, therefore, treated as human subjects whose feedback is essential to the accuracy of the assessment. . . .

> Externally designed and externally mandated tests are dangerously immune to the possibility that a student might legitimately need to have a question rephrased or might deserve the opportunity to defend an unexpected or "incorrect" answer. . . . To gauge understanding, we must explore a student's answer; there must be some possibility of dialogue between the assessor and the assessed to insure that the student is fully examined. (708)

There is much in the news today about creating a national standardized test based on national education goals. While this goal is admirable, in reality it will not work given the ideas we have been discussing in this book. Emily Grady (1992) makes the following observation:

> National standardized tests have been proposed as a primary strategy for education reform. However, standardized tests will not improve education. They do not provide useful information for educating children; they may lack validity and reliability in what they attempt to assess; they drive the curriculum in harmful ways; they lead to unfair labeling; and they discriminate among races and between genders. The rising tide of testing in the United States in the past few years threatens to drown us in useless statistics.
>
> Education needs accountability, but accountability must contribute to the growth of students. Assessment needs to be based in the classroom. Teachers must be central to the assessment process; they must be the documenters and reviewers of their students' learning. Students must enter into the assessment process in order to gain insight and confidence in controlling their own learning. . . .
>
> Instead of national standardized tests, there should be a national agenda to establish criteria that guide student learning. (29)

Unless the standards of this national standardized test allow students to demonstrate their academic success in a variety of ways that include at least the seven intelligences, and unless they take into account a developmentally appropriate understanding of students, they are flawed from the start and will serve only to perpetuate the existing biases that are blatantly unfair to both students and teachers. The new standards must include both the development of intelligence capacities as well as mastery of the academic curriculum.

Multiple Intelligence Approaches to Assessment © 1994 Zephyr Press, Tucson, Arizona

New Standards: What Should We Be Looking For?

We must begin the process of building a consensus on the common learnings and processes students need to master in the various subject areas of the curriculum at the various levels of their development and growth as human beings. These new criteria must go way beyond (but include) the verbal-linguistic and logical-mathematical biases of the past (the famous/infamous "basics"; namely, reading, writing, and 'rithmetic). Our concern as a society should be to help students attain mastery and understanding of these common learnings and processes. Creating these new standards will necessarily involve educators from all grade levels and academic disciplines, as well as members of the business community, parents, and other concerned people from the local community. And we must remember that, given the reality of the knowledge explosion, it is quite possible that an understanding of the process dimension of the various academic disciplines is as important as the content!

Once we have developed a consensus of what is worth knowing, teaching, and learning, we must integrate thoroughly the assessment process as part of the curriculum, not as something that occurs alongside of or separate from the instruction. In fact, *if the tests are authentic,* they should be at the heart of instruction and of maintaining high standards in our schools. Grant Wiggins (1988) puts it this way: "'Teaching to the test' is a dirty phrase only when the test lacks integrity as a standard-setting intellectual challenge and when teachers have no hand in setting the standards of design and scoring. In all genuine learning, the student is continually confronted with the 'tests' and challenges at the heart of the activity or discipline: all coaches happily teach to the 'test' of performance" (29).

As I have repeatedly tried to point out in this book, just because students can produce something on a written test does not mean they really know the material. It is possible they were simply lucky in producing correct answers on a given day! Or it may mean simply that they are skilled in recalling various bits of memorized information. And vice versa: just because they don't do well doesn't mean they don't know the material. It may mean they had a bad day or that they ate too much sugar at breakfast. It could also mean that they did not understand the structure, form, and process of the test (and of course, once the formal test begins, everyone knows no talking is allowed, let alone questioning of the test itself!). When students fail these kinds of inauthentic tests, we should be asking who has really failed—the students or the test?

If we are really concerned with students' deep understanding of what they are learning in school, I believe we must provide them with opportunities to be examined in a wide variety of ways on the same information (see chapter 6 on "multiperceptual testing" for suggestions on how to do this), all with the purpose of giving them opportunities to "show off" what they have learned—to demonstrate or "perform" their understanding—rather than using testing as occasions to tell them where they have failed and what they don't know.

Authentic Assessment: Toward a Definition

There is a great deal in the literature today about "authentic assessment." A consensus is rapidly emerging of what makes a given assessment authentic versus inauthentic. In the context of this writing, I would like to suggest that what we also need is intelligence-based assessment. Intelligence-based assessment suggests an evaluation process that is brain-compatible and that applies state-of-the-art brain/mind research to the examination process. Today we know more about how to tap the untapped potentials of the human brain/mind/body system than humans have ever known before. It is high time we start acting on this knowledge!

The same thing can be said about the findings of current educational research; we know more about teaching and learning than humans have ever known. This educational research base is immense and includes such things as methods for improving student thinking skills and cognitive abilities, new instructional practices that educate the whole child, integrated and inter-disciplinary approaches to curriculum design and implementation, collaborative teaching and cooperative learning processes for increased student understanding, and teaching for the transfer of learning beyond the classroom into practical everyday living. In the following chapter I have spelled out my vision of intelligence-based assessment, including theoretical guidelines for designing such assessments, specific testing instruments and techniques, and suggestions for applying these instruments to the various academic areas. My task in the remainder of this chapter is to attempt to notch some trees, so to speak, on some of the theoretical/practical factors involved in creating authentic, intelligence-based assessments.

Howard Gardner (1993) proposes that an authentic assessment must occur in context, much like what occurs in an apprenticeship situation, where the apprentice must demonstrate ability to perform skills of a particular craft. Gardner calls this the "apprentice model" of assessment, which stands in bold relief against the current, popular "formal testing" model:

> [The two models] may be said to represent two extremes. The first "formal testing" model is conceived of as an objective, decontextualized form of assessment, which can be adopted and implemented widely with some assurance that similar results will be obtained. The second "apprenticeship model" is implemented almost entirely within a naturally occurring context in which the particularities of a craft are embedded. The assessment is based upon a prior analysis of the skills involved in a particular craft, but it may also be influenced by subjective factors, including the master's personal views about his apprentice, his relationship with other masters, or his need for other kinds of services. . . .
>
> Our society has embraced the formal testing model to an excessive degree; I contend that aspects of the apprentice model of learning and assessment—which I term "contextualized learning"—would be profitably reintroduced into our education system. (162–63)

Grant Wiggins (1989) defines authentic assessment as assessment in which students must perform exemplary tasks that are typically required when one has mastered a particular discipline. In light of this authenticity Wiggins proposes that academic tests should be the intellectual and academic equivalent of the public performances that take place in such areas as athletics or the fine arts (for example, a musical recital or a showing of one's paintings or sculpture).

In *How to Assess Thoughtful Outcomes*, Kay Burke (1993) presents the following list of definitions and phrases from the work of T. Stefonek (1991), which summarize the thinking of various experts in the field. These can help delineate some of the dynamics and factors that should be present in an authentic assessment.

- Methods that emphasize learning and thinking, especially higher-order thinking skills such as problem-solving strategies (Collins)

- Tasks that focus on students' ability to produce a quality product or performance (Wiggins)

- Disciplined inquiry that integrates and produces knowledge, rather than reproduces fragments of information others have discovered (Newmann)

- Meaningful tasks at which students should learn to excel (Wiggins)

- Challenges that require knowledge in good use and good judgment (Wiggins)

- A new type of positive interaction between the assessor and assessee (Wiggins)

- An examination of differences between trivial school tasks (e.g., giving definitions of biological terms) and more meaningful performance in nonschool settings (e.g., completing a field survey of wildlife) (Newmann)

- Involvement that demystifies tasks and standards (Wiggins)

Burke (1993) also includes the following thoughts, which provide further definition of authentic assessment:

> Regardless of the different terminology, most of the various definitions exhibit two central features: "First, all are viewed as *alternatives* to traditional multiple-choice, standardardized achievement tests; second, all refer to *direct* examination of student *performance* on significant tasks that are relevant to life outside of school" (Worthen 1993, 445).
>
> Authentic assessment means many things to many people, but Archibald and Newmann perhaps say it best: "A valid assessment systems provides information about the particular tasks on which students succeed or fail, but more important, it also presents tasks that are worthwhile, significant, and meaningful—in short, *authentic*" (Archibald and Newmann 1988, 1).

Benchmarks of Authenticity: Guidelines for Designing Authentic, Intelligence-Based Tests

Four major assumptions underlie the guidelines I am suggesting for designing authentic tests: (1) tests should be formative, that is, designed in such as way as to reveal, elicit, beckon, cajole, and evoke students' strengths (many of which may be latent); (2) tests should provide students with a wide variety of contextualized opportunities to "show off," demonstrate, or perform what they know; (3) tests should be of genuine benefit to students and promote further intellectual and cognitive development by enhancing, deepening, and expanding their understanding of themselves, the various academic disciplines, and the world in which we live; and (4) tests should accommodate the full spectrum of the intelligences, allowing students choices based on how they feel they can demonstrate that they have mastered the required material. Howard Gardner (1988) sums up these points as follows: "Assessment programs that fail to take into account the vast differences among individuals, developmental levels, and varieties of expertise are increasingly anachronistic. Formal testing could, in principle, be adjusted to take these documented variations into account. But it would require a suspension of some of the key assumptions of standardized testing, such as uniformity of individuals in key respects and the penchant for cost-efficient instruments." (177)

The following charts suggest a schema for moving toward designing authentic, intelligence-based assessments of students' academic progress. The charts address three major areas of concern in restructuring current assessment practices:

- The structure, form, and logistics of examinations (the HOW and WHERE of testing)

- The academic design of examinations (the WHAT is really worth testing)

- The grading and scoring of examinations (the WHY of testing)

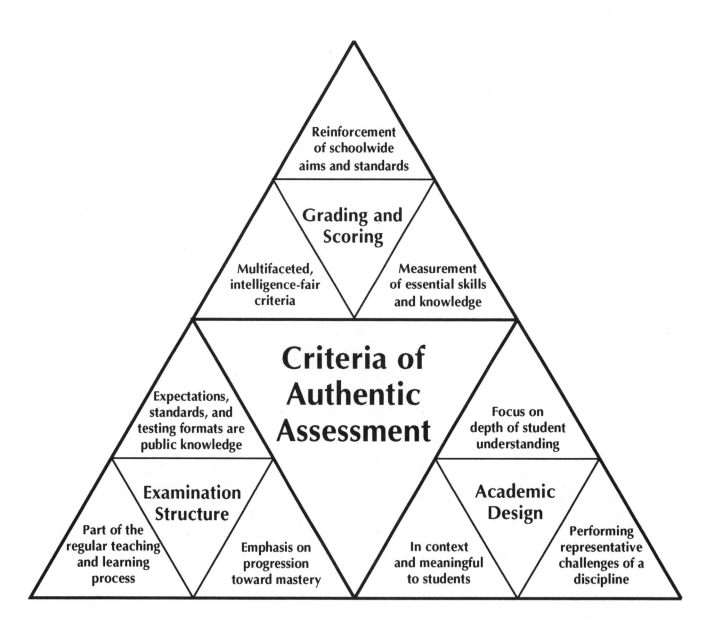

 Multiple Intelligence Approaches to Assessment © 1994 Zephyr Press, Tucson, Arizona

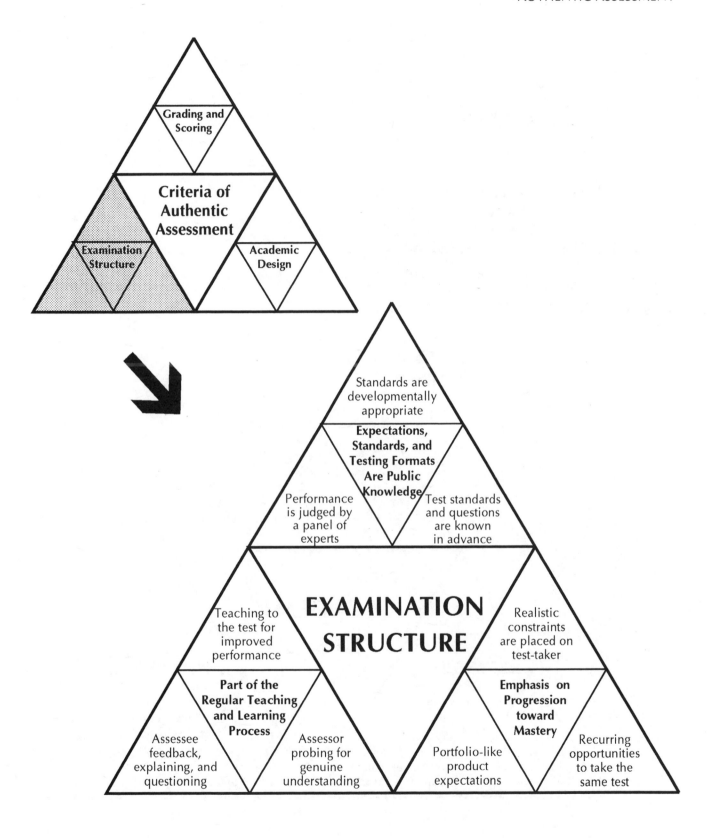

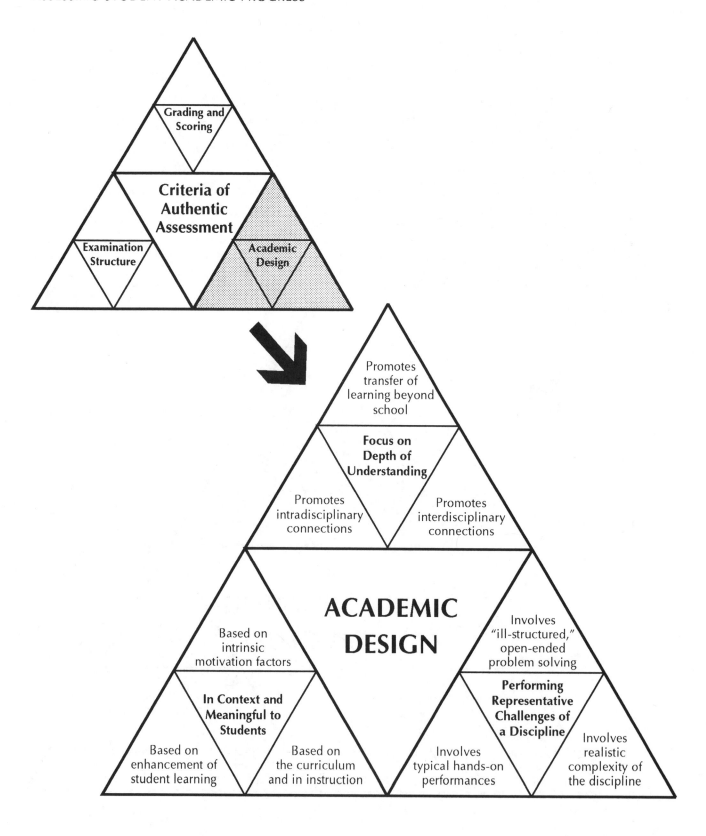

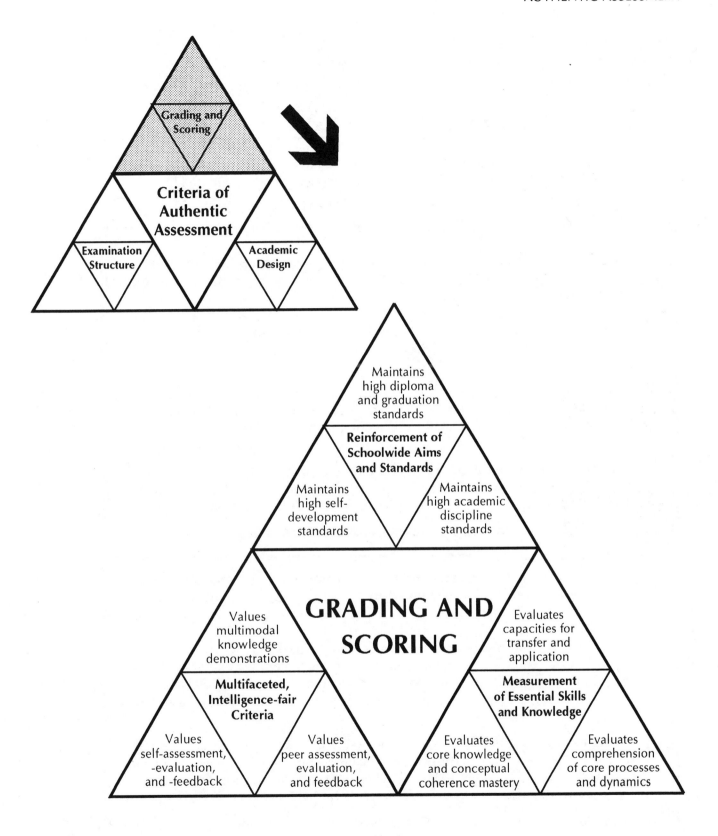

Benchmarks for Authenticity: Guidelines for Designing Authentic, Intelligence-Based Tests

Following is an explanation of the information contained on the preceding triangle charts.

EXAMINATION STRUCTURE

These factors involve the dynamic interaction between the students, the assessor, the assessment instruments, and the larger community, including its concern with holding schools accountable to agreed-upon graduation standards.

Authentic, intelligence-fair assessment is **part of the regular teaching and learning process** as opposed to something that occurs at special times and places, apart from and isolated from daily instruction:

★ **Assessee feedback, explaining, and questioning.** Students are encouraged to become active participants in convincing the assessor that they have indeed mastered the required material.

★ **Assessor probing for genuine understanding.** The major concern of those administering an examination is to enter a genuine dialogue with students to discern fully the students' knowledge base, skill level, and understanding of the processes within a particular discipline.

★ **Teaching to the test for improved performance.** Students should know beforehand what will be on an examination, and instruction should be tailored to helping them fully demonstrate their knowledge and improve their performances.

Authentic, intelligence-fair assessment places its **emphasis on progression toward mastery** of the various content and knowledge components, processes, and dynamics of a particular academic discipline:

★ **Portfolio-like product expectations.** Students are enabled and given an opportunity to keep a record of their learning, including examples of their best work, of how their skill in a given discipline has progressed over time, and of how their self-concept has changed; this practice gives a fuller picture of students' work as opposed to isolated examples.

★ **Recurring opportunities to take the same test.** Examinations are developmentally spiraled and represent a variety of stages of achievement (content, process, skill, and so on); they are worth taking and worth repeating until students master the material.

★ **Realistic constraints are placed on the test-taker.** The constraints of the examination are similar to those encountered in the field when the discipline to be tested shows up outside of formal education.

EXAMINATION STRUCTURE *(continued)*

Authentic, intelligence-fair assessment ensures that the **examination expectations, standards, and testing formats are public knowledge**, are known to both students and parents, and that the community at large is involved in the assessment process:

★ **Performance is judged by a panel of experts.** Students' performances on examinations are evaluated by experts in the various disciplines (including teachers!), very similar to how athletes are judged in the Olympics.

★ **Test standards and questions are known in advance.** Examinations are based on a consensus regarding the core knowledge, process knowledge, and skills and aptitudes necessary for the various disciplines.

★ **Standards are developmentally appropriate.** Examinations are designed to help students move from the novice level of knowledge, understanding, and skill development in a discipline to the level of mastery, very similar to what occurs in an apprenticeship program.

Benchmarks of Authenticity: Guidelines for
Designing Authentic, Intelligence-Based Tests *(continued)*

ACADEMIC DESIGN ——————————

These factors involve motivating students to master the skills and capacities of a variety
of disciplines and ensuring that students gain deeper understanding of the various
academic disciplines, versus the ability merely to recall series of memorized facts.

Authentic, intelligence-fair assessment **occurs in context and is meaningful to
students**; thus students look forward to assessment occasions because the practices
give students an opportunity to show off what they know and can do:

★ **Based on enhancement of student learning.** The purpose of any and all assessments should be to benefit students by promoting understanding and challenging
them to ever higher levels of achievement.

★ **Based ON the curriculum and IN instruction.** Any and all assessments are
directly related to the actual curriculum of the school and district, are designed
by those who are responsible for teaching the curriculum, and match the various
instructional practices used in the teaching and learning situation.

★ **Based on intrinsic motivation factors.** The motivation for doing well on a test
is within the test itself; that is, the test is worth taking for its own sake and thus
students want to improve their performance each time they take the test. Students
in essence compete with themselves.

Authentic, intelligence-fair assessment involves students in the **performing of
representative challenges of a discipline** as those challenges show up in the so-called
real world, where the discipline is actually being practiced. Assessment tools are
modeled after performances in such things as sports, music recitals, and theatrical
performances:

★ **Involves typical hands-on performances.** Students are asked to perform the kinds
of tasks, use various processes, and understand the knowledge of a particular
discipline that will be encountered in the pursuit of vocations and avocations
typical of the discipline in life beyond school.

★ **Involves realistic complexity of the discipline.** Examinations are designed to
allow students to demonstrate higher-order thinking, synthesis, and integration
of what they have learned; assessments are thus appropriately graduated to allow
demonstration of basic, intermediate, and advanced levels of mastery.

★ **Involves "ill-structured," open-ended problem-solving.** Students' ability to think
creatively through a problem is valued as much as getting the so-called right answer; there are often several right answers. Successful performance is directly linked
to students' being able to defend and to explain how they arrived at answers.

ACADEMIC DESIGN *(continued)*

Authentic, intelligence-fair assessment is **focused on depth of understanding** as opposed to simple recall of information on multiple choice, fill-in-the-blank, or essay tests that seek regurgitation of information but minimal grasp of the meaning of a variety of facts, figures, and data:

★ **Promotes intradisciplinary connections.** Assessment helps students understand how their acquired knowledge relates to, enhances, and can be used in other aspects and dimensions of the particular discipline being studied.

★ **Promotes interdisciplinary connections.** Assessment helps students understand how their acquired knowledge relates to, enhances, and can be utilized in other disciplines of the curriculum they are studying in their formal education.

★ **Promotes transfer of learning beyond school.** Students' understanding of and faculties of practical application of what they have learned in school are seen as the true test of understanding.

Benchmarks of Authenticity: Guidelines for
Designing Authentic, Intelligence-Based Tests *(continued)*

GRADING AND SCORING
LOGISTICS AND PRACTICES _____

These factors involve the maintenance of high academic standards, ensuring that tests
are by design intelligence fair and that test scores accurately reflect students' knowledge
base.

Authentic, intelligence-fair assessment is concerned with **multifaceted, intelligence-fair criteria** that take into account the fact that all students do not learn in the same way
and that in order to report adequately and fairly on students' progress, assessment tools
must consider a wide variety of factors:

★ **Values self-assessment, -evaluation, and -feedback.** Students are required to
reflect on and evaluate their own performance on formal examinations and are
encouraged to discuss their performance with and provide input to the assessor.

★ **Values peer assessment, evaluation, and feedback.** Students are given opportunities to be assessed and examined by their peers and to receive feedback from their
peers regarding their performance on a given assessment, including suggestions on
how they might improve their performance next time.

★ **Values multiperceptual knowledge demonstrations.** Students are given opportunities and are required to demonstrate their knowledge and understanding in a wide
variety of ways. Students understand that their success on one kind of test does not
necessarily mean they genuinely understand or have mastered the necessary material.

Authentic, intelligence-fair assessment is concerned with **mastery and measurement of the essential skills and knowledge** of a particular discipline as opposed to
the relative nonessentials, which are often emphasized at the expense of focusing on
students' mastery of the foundation of a discipline:

★ **Evaluates core knowledge and conceptual coherence mastery.** The concern is
to discern students' working knowledge of a discipline in a holistic and integrated
way, as opposed to rewarding their ability to recall bits and pieces of knowledge
disconnected from and not related to the discipline as a whole.

★ **Evaluates comprehension of core processes and dynamics.** The focus is to
appraise students' ability to utilize skillfully the various critical skills, processes,
and competencies involved in a given discipline in an integrated, well-orchestrated
manner as opposed to the fragmented use of the discipline out of context.

★ **Evaluates capacities for transfer and application.** Assessment of students' ability
to transfer or apply learning across the curriculum, to other subject areas, and into
real-life situations is valued more than learning that can be demonstrated only in
special testing situations, but with little understanding of its relevance.

GRADING AND SCORING
LOGISTICS AND PRACTICES *(continued)*

Authentic, intelligence-fair assessment is concerned with the **reinforcement of schoolwide aims and standards**, including the individual and personal developmental journey of students and the academic standards of the school and district; assessment is at the center of one's education:

★ **Maintains high self-development standards.** Students are expected and encouraged to set academic achievement goals for themselves; assessments are occasions for them to evaluate and monitor their progress toward attaining these personal development objectives.

★ **Maintains high academic discipline standards.** The assessment instruments and practices promote high academic standards because everyone knows what is required to achieve mastery, and tests are designed to move students systematically toward the realization of the mastery level in each discipline.

★ **Maintains high diploma and graduation standards.** The "testing journey" is constructed to help students fulfill the requirements for graduation by giving students examinations that challenge them to ever-increasing levels of complexity, understanding, and mastery with each successive examination.

6

Multiperceptual Formal Testing

Assessing Student Academic Progress

(Models for Change)

In this chapter I offer some practical assessment models that move toward establishing a variety of new instruments for evaluating students' academic progress. The first supposition behind these suggestions is that our testing practices must take into account a developmentally appropriate approach to teaching and learning. The key research behind this supposition is Jerome Bruner's (1956) pioneering work on the "spiral curriculum." In a nutshell, Bruner states that a teacher can teach *anything* to *anybody* at *any age* **if** the teacher takes the time to crawl inside the worldview of the student and speak the language that is meaningful to the student at the given stage in the student's development.

The second supposition behind the suggestions I give here is that, assuming our concern is genuine understanding as opposed to simple attainment of knowledge, assessment must be multiperceptual. The new assessment practices must involve at least seven ways of knowing, understanding, perceiving, and learning. Dr. Jean Houston (1980) calls this learning "multiperceptual learning":

> In order to preserve the genius and developmental potential of childhood, one must quite simply give the universe back to the child, in as rich and dramatic a form as possible.
>
> Multiperceptual learning, we have found, is a key to this gifting. In school curricula and programs . . . the child is taught to think in images as well as in words, to learn spelling or even arithmetic in rhythmic patterns, to think with his/her whole body—in short, to learn school subjects, and more from a much larger spectrum of sensory and cognitive possibilities. (84)

I suggest that, in order to be fair and holistically accurate in our assessment of students' academic progress, we must move to multiperceptual testing in our schools. In *Seven Ways of Knowing* (Lazear 1991) I made the following observation about intelligence testing: "The key to designing tests for assessing different types of intelligence is that each test must itself be presented in the language and symbol system of the intelligence it purports to test. For example, a test that is presented verbally cannot accurately test for bodily-kinesthetic intelligence, even if one is able to describe a physical activity in minute detail! The 'language' or symbol system of bodily-kinesthetic intelligence is physical movement itself and thus the test must be presented in these terms" (175).

I believe the same applies to the assessment of students' academic progress; namely, in order to give students the opportunity to demonstrate the fullness of their knowledge, we must ask them to show us what they know in a wide variety of ways through tests that are couched in the unique language of each intelligence. Linda Campbell, Dee Dickinson, and Bruce Campbell make the following point in *Teaching and Learning through Multiple Intelligences*: "Just as students benefit from learning in many ways, they also benefit from demonstrating their knowledge in more than one way. . . . some students who are weaker in the linguistic and mathematical domains may find it easier to share what they know through charting, a role-play, or in song. All students may find multiple assessment options motivating and interesting, thus extending their learning through the assessment process" (120).

Following are some beginning ideas for experimenting with intelligence-fair tests that go beyond but include the biases of the traditional assessments toward verbal-linguistic and logical-mathematical skills.

Intelligence-Based Assessment Guidelines

The Multiple Intelligence Assessment Menu (p. 111) presents a palette of suggestions around which different kinds of tests can be created. These tests should be designed to provide opportunities for all students to demonstrate their knowledge and learning in a variety of ways based on the multiple intelligences. Invite students to help create different kinds of tests that they believe will allow them to demonstrate what they have learned. Make the students responsible for proving, in and through a given test, that they have mastered the required material in whatever ways they can. Remember, each test must be couched in the language, jargon, vernacular, mode, and media of the specific intelligence it purports to test.

To underscore one of my presuppositions once again: a student's performing successfully on a given test does not necessarily demonstrate genuine learning or understanding; it may tell us only who is good at taking that type of test. A multiperceptual approach to testing can help us tailor our teaching practice to expand and amplify students' knowledge base from a whole-learning perspective. The task is then ours to teach students how to transfer their learning so they can do well on the various standardized tests our society currently deems important. We must expand the bases of testing to include all of the intelligences to get a true perspective of genuine learning and understanding. Although covering all these bases is key to assessing whether students have truly mastered a concept or skill, you need not cover them all in a single test. On the following pages, each suggested assessment instrument on the Multiple Intelligence Assessment Instruments Menu is described, and suggestions for its application to different subject areas are provided.

Multiple Intelligence Assessment Menu

Verbal-Linguistic Intelligence
(Language Arts–Based Assessment Instruments)

- written essays
- vocabulary quizzes
- recall of verbal information
- audiocassette recordings
- poetry writing
- linguistic humor
- formal speech
- cognitive debates
- listening and reporting
- learning logs and journals

Logical-Mathematical Intelligence
(Cognitive Patterns–Based Assessment Instruments)

- cognitive organizers
- higher-order reasoning
- pattern games
- outlining
- logic and rationality exercises
- mental menus and formulas
- deductive reasoning
- inductive reasoning
- calculation processes
- logical analysis and critique

Visual-Spatial Intelligence
(Imaginal-Based Assessment Instruments)

- murals and montages
- graphic representation and visual illustrating
- visualization and imagination
- reading, understanding, and creating maps
- flowcharts and graphs
- sculpting and building
- imaginary conversations
- mind mapping
- video recording and photography
- manipulative demonstrations

Bodily-Kinesthetic Intelligence
(Performance-Based Assessment Instruments)

- lab experiments
- dramatization
- original and classical dance
- charades and mimes
- impersonations
- human tableaux
- invention projects
- physical exercise routines and games
- skill demonstrations
- illustrations using body language and gestures

Musical-Rhythmic Intelligence
(Auditory-Based Assessment Instruments)

- creating concept songs and raps
- illustrating with sound
- discerning rhythmic patterns
- composing music
- linking music and rhythm with concepts
- orchestrating music
- creating percussion patterns
- recognizing tonal patterns and quality
- analyzing musical structure
- reproducing musical and rhythmic patterns

Interpersonal Intelligence
(Relational-Based Assessment Instruments)

- group "jigsaws"
- explaining to or teaching another
- "think-pair-share"
- "round robin"
- giving and receiving feedback
- interviews, question-naires, and people searches
- empathic processing
- random group quizzes
- assess your teammates
- test, coach, and retest

Intrapersonal Intelligence
(Psychological-Based Assessment Instruments)

- autobiographical reporting
- personal application scenarios
- metacognitive surveys and questionnaires
- higher-order questions and answers
- concentration tests
- feelings diaries and logs
- personal projection
- self-identification reporting
- personal history correlation
- personal priorities and goals

Verbal-Linguistic Intelligence

Language Arts–Based Assessment

Language arts–based assessment asks students to demonstrate their knowledge and learning through effective linguistic communication. The primary mode of this form of assessment is the written and spoken language, including such things as essays and reports, formal and impromptu conversation, dialogues, creative writing, and comprehension of reading.

These tests should require students to use the specific capacities of verbal-linguistic intelligence: understanding the order and meaning of words; convincing someone to take a course of action; explaining and teaching something to someone else; learning something from another's instructions, through written or spoken humor, memory, and recall; and metalinguistic analysis (using language to investigate language).

Students must be able to communicate their learning and knowledge in and through proper grammar, syntax, phonetics, and the praxis of a formal language system.

Assessment Instruments

- **written essays**—using a variety of forms and sentence styles (declarative, interrogative, descriptive and so on) to demonstrate one's knowledge of a topic
- **vocabulary quizzes**—showing recognition, understanding, correct pronunciation, and proper usage of vocabulary words
- **recall of verbal information**—using verbal games, puzzles, and question-and-answer activities to recall information studied or learned
- **audiocassette recording**—verbalizing the best answers, thinking processes, and related ideas on an audiocassette
- **poetry writing**—expressing understanding in verse and through various kinds of rhyming patterns
- **linguistic humor**—making jokes, riddles, and plays on words about various subjects and concepts being learned or studied
- **formal speech**—making formal presentations involving public speaking about something learned
- **cognitive debates**—demonstrating knowledge of a subject by defending opinions or taking a side opposite to one's own opinions
- **listening and reporting**—listening to presentations and then reporting what was learned
- **learning logs and journals**—keeping a written record of the growth of one's own knowledge and understanding in a given subject area

---

Verbal-Linguistic Assessment Ideas

LANGUAGE ARTS	HISTORY	MATHEMATICS	SCIENCE/HEALTH
★ Demonstrate ability to express one's thoughts, feelings, and ideas in and through writing	★ Use storytelling to explain a historical event or the causes of an event	★ Write accurate math story problems for another to solve	★ Give a verbal report on a scientific experiment
★ Make up a story that shows understanding of grammar, syntax, semantics, and the praxis of the language	★ Use crossword puzzles and word jumbles to recall historical facts and figures	★ Explain to another how to solve certain math problems and perform certain operations	★ Invent a set of slogans that show understanding of various healthy living practices
★ Set up a debate between characters in a story; debate the pros and cons of a thought expressed in an essay or a poem	★ Recognize historical periods through the poetry, drama, and literature of the period	★ Analyze the linguistic structure of a problem to find clues to its solution	★ Make an outline for a TV sitcom, detective story, or soap opera in which the main characters are various scientific processes
★ Make an audiocassette recording that explains your reflections or thoughts about something you have read	★ Design a newspaper that might have been created by people living in a certain historical era	★ Create limericks to demonstrate understanding of various math concepts and processes	★ Create puns, jokes, or riddles based on scientific vocabulary words
★ In your own words, retell a story you have read or tell it as if it had happened in today's world	★ Write an imaginary interview with key historical figures, including your questions and their likely responses	★ Create a TV talk show in which the guests must solve math problems	★ Create written reports that summarize the results of health surveys or science experiments
★ Create limericks or other humorus rhymes about such things as parts of speech, parts of a sentence, stages of the writing process, and so on	★ Conduct a debate between historical figures who were on opposite sides of an issue	★ Make up a series of math process and operation riddles	★ Make up a science or health terms or processes word game (for example, a crossword or a word jumble)

Multiple Intelligence Approaches to Assessment © 1994 Zephyr Press, Tucson, Arizona

Verbal-Linguistic
Assessment Ideas *(continued)*

GLOBAL STUDIES	LIFE SKILLS	FINE ARTS

GLOBAL STUDIES

★ Demonstrate cultural knowledge through creative writing exercises

★ Recognize different cultures through their literary forms (for example, haiku, sonnets, epic poetry)

★ Write a letter to someone in another culture, then write what you think his or her response might be

★ Conduct a class discussion about a current affairs issue that deals with different points of view

★ Interview people in a culture other than your own and make a written or spoken presentation of what you have learned

★ Demonstrate understanding of language idioms from different cultures

LIFE SKILLS

★ *Home arts:* Demonstrate ability to read, comprehend, and follow a recipe or directions for making something

★ *Driver's education:* Demonstrate understanding of the names and functions of different parts of an automobile, including the engine

★ *Industrial arts:* Demonstrate the ability to translate verbal instructions into the performance of a task or the creation of something

★ *Computer science:* Show understanding of various computer jargon (for example, verbal menus, error messages, commands, hardware, software)

★ *Physical education:* Explain to others how to perform a physical feat, task, or activity

FINE ARTS

★ Write poetry to express an idea, opinion, feeling, or belief

★ Write an essay about your responses to and thoughts about a play, film, or TV show

★ Write the instructions for performing a dance routine you have created or that you know

★ Create a painting, sculpture, or drawing that communicates the ideas and feelings about something you have read

★ Change the lyrics of a song so they reflect an idea, opinion, feeling, or belief you hold

★ Write the script for an original drama or role-play (including stage directions and set descriptions)

Logical-Mathematical Intelligence

Cognitive Patterns–Based Assessment

Cognitive patterns–based assessment asks students to show what they have learned through logical and analytical thought processes. The primary mode of this type of assessment is finding, recognizing, and using patterns, including abstract number patterns, word patterns, or more concrete, object-based visual and tactile patterns.

These tests should require students to use the specific capacities of logical-mathematical intelligence: abstract pattern recognition, inductive and deductive reasoning, discerning logical relationships and connections, performance of varieties of complex calculations, and scientific reasoning.

Students must be able to demonstrate their learning and knowledge by solving different kinds of subject-related problems and explaining various patterns and rationales of the specific content being tested.

Assessment Instruments

- **cognitive organizers**—using various thinking pattern maps, such as webs, Venn diagrams, and classification matrixes to demonstrate understanding or knowledge of a subject

- **higher-order reasoning**—moving from factual recall, through process, to understanding, to synthesis and integration when thinking about or learning something

- **pattern games**—demonstrating understanding of a subject through recognition or reproduction of its patterns

- **outlining**—showing grasp of a subject by listing main points, subpoints, subpoints of the subpoints, and so on

- **logic and rationality exercises**—exhibiting understanding and knowledge through various kinds of syllogisms or "if . . . then . . . " statements

- **mental menus and formulas**—using acrostics, acronyms, and other kinds of formulas to prove knowledge of a subject or topic

- **deductive reasoning**—showing ability to sort or classify specific information into general categories within a subject

- **inductive reasoning**—showing ability to reach conclusions or create general categories based on specific details of a subject

- **calculation processes**—exhibiting understanding by employing various problem-solving strategies related to an area of study

- **logical analysis and critique**—demonstrating knowledge of a subject area by applying criteria such as literary criticism or the scientific method

---

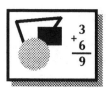

Logical-Mathematical Assessment Ideas

LANGUAGE ARTS	HISTORY	MATHEMATICS	SCIENCE/HEALTH
★ Show understanding of the logical patterns of the language (for example, grammar and syntax)	★ Grasp the causes and effects of historical events	★ Demonstrate understanding of how to perform various mathematic operations	★ Demonstrate understanding of the dynamics involved in various scientific processes (for example, digestion, photosynthesis, states of matter)
★ Demonstrate a grasp of the steps of the writing process	★ Demonstrate ability to analyze historical trends and to make predictions	★ Demonstrate knowledge of problem-solving steps in a variety of situations, including traditional math problems	★ Classify inductively and deductively scientific processes and information
★ Demonstrate ability to analyze logically a piece of literature, including character, plot, setting, and so on	★ Demonstrate understanding of key contributions of various historical figures	★ Make up story problems that are based on real life situations for another to solve	★ Interpret the meaning of various data from an experiment
★ Demonstrate knowledge of how to prepare and deliver a variety of effective formal speeches	★ Create a time line of the key events of a period in history	★ Translate the steps of solving a problem into a symbolic formula	★ Outline the detailed steps for setting up a science lab experiment
★ Hypothesize about what might have happened in a story if certain factors were different	★ Demonstrate ability to analyze historical trends for causal relationships	★ Predict and justify the answer to a problem before solving it, then solve it and evaluate the predictions	★ Predict the results of a health survey, then conduct the survey and evaluate your predictions
★ Rearrange jumbled words or sentences to make a comprehensible sentence or paragraph	★ Show understanding by comparing and contrasting different periods of history	★ Create a matrix that classifies different kinds of mathematical processes and operations	★ Make up a trivia game about healthy lifestyles

Multiple Intelligence Approaches to Assessment © 1994 Zephyr Press, Tucson, Arizona

Logical-Mathematical
Assessment Ideas *(continued)*

GLOBAL STUDIES	LIFE SKILLS	FINE ARTS

GLOBAL STUDIES

★ Compare and contrast key features of different cultures

★ Demonstrate understanding of the relationship of environmental factors to social development

★ Interpret the meaning of various behaviors from different cultural perspectives

★ Recognize location on a map from various geographical patterns and factors

★ Create a "Guess My Culture" clue game

★ Interpret the meaning of various symbolic information on a map that has no legend

LIFE SKILLS

★ *Home arts:* Create a logical system for organizing recipes, a tool closet, or a file cabinet, or make a calendar of upcoming events for you and your family

★ *Driver's education:* Give a rationale for the rules of the road and list the basics of caring for an automobile (short and long term)

★ *Industrial arts:* Explain how to operate safely and care for various machines and tools; be sure to tell why the procedures are important

★ *Computer science:* Create an "if . . . then . . . " chart showing what the computer will do if you do "x"

★ *Physical education:* Demonstrate knowledge of the rules of various sports and the step-by-step techniques for the execution of different motor skills

FINE ARTS

★ Show recognition of key patterns of an artist's style

★ Demonstrate understanding of the basic language of music (for example, signature, notation, rhythm)

★ Demonstrate knowledge of the steps of a variety of dances

★ Demonstrate the ability to recognize various artistic techniques (for example, perspective, cubism, surrealism, impressionism)

★ Demonstrate ability to recognize various musical techniques and instruments

★ Create an original poem from randomly selected data on a matrix

Visual-Spatial Intelligence

Imaginal-Based Assessment

Imaginal-based assessment asks students to create visual displays and mental images through which their knowledge and learning can be evaluated. The primary mode of this form of assessment is the visual arts, including such things as painting, drawing, sculpting, imagination, and work with various kinds of hands-on manipulatives, as well as processes for seeing with the mind's eye.

The test should require students to use specific capacities related to visual-spatial intelligence: active imagination, forming mental images, graphic representation, finding one's way in space, recognizing relationships of objects, image manipulations, and perception of objects from different angles.

Students must be able to demonstrate their learning and knowledge in the language and media of visual perception, namely, using images, designs, colors, textures, pictures, and visual symbols, patterns, designs, and shapes.

Assessment Instruments

- **murals and montages**—creating a collection of images and pictures that show understanding of certain material
- **graphic representation and visual illustrating**—drawing something or creating illustrations to show aspects, dynamics, or relationships within a topic
- **visualization and imagination**—using the active imagination to create pictures in the mind about things being studied and then describing what is being seen
- **reading, understanding, and creating maps**—creating legends to communicate spatial information or following directions on a map
- **flowcharts and graphs**—showing steps of various processes or operations, or presenting research findings from a project
- **sculpting and building**—constructing physical models that demonstrate stages of a process or inventing something based on learned concepts
- **imaginary conversations**—interviewing figures and characters from daily lessons or pretending to have conversations with various concepts or processes
- **mind mapping**—expressing understanding through visual maps that show color, images, and relationships within something being studied
- **video recording and photography**—reporting on field research for a project or taking photos that illustrate understanding or certain ideas
- **manipulative demonstrations**—working with various physical objects to show understanding of a concept or idea

Visual-Spatial Assessment Ideas

LANGUAGE ARTS	HISTORY	MATHEMATICS	SCIENCE/HEALTH
★ Visualize and draw scenes and characters from literature (that is, represent graphically what is seen in the mind's eye)	★ Recognize in pictures the various scenes, events, and figures from history	★ Demonstrate understanding of mathematical concepts using manipulatives	★ Draw or sculpt what was observed under a microscope or during an experiment
★ Create posters and brochures to explain such things as the writing process and rules of grammar	★ Demonstrate understanding of various historical periods through creation of visual art forms (for example, murals, dioramas, collages, montages)	★ Recognize various kinds of numerical patterns in pictures	★ Demonstrate understanding of various scientific processes by constructing a model and demonstrating its operation
★ Demonstrate understanding of syntax using linguistic manipulatives (for example, manipulating words in sentences to create new meanings or flash cards with pictures to express vocabulary)	★ Recognize the costumes, works of art, architecture, and so on, of various historical periods	★ Create graphs and charts of various mathematical data (for example, the results of a survey, statistical comparisons, factors of a story problem)	★ Create flowcharts to show how to perform a scientific experiment
★ Show reading comprehension through explaining or answering questions about pictures from or about something read	★ Make flowcharts to show historical factors that led to a significant historical event	★ Design bulletin boards that show the flow of performing different mathematical operations	★ Create posters that present various health and science findings to others in a compelling manner
★ Graph the dramatic flow of a story, a play, a paragraph, and so on	★ Have imaginary conversations with persons from the past	★ Form various geometric shapes with string or wet noodles	★ Have an imaginary conversation with various parts of the body
★ Mind map the rules of grammar, the writing process, and so on	★ Create travel poster ads for visiting various periods of history	★ Invent a board game that incorporates understanding of different math concepts	★ Code with color various stages and dynamics of a scientific process
	★ Make graphs of various historical developments (such as inventions, ideas, and so on)		

Visual-Spatial
Assessment Ideas *(continued)*

GLOBAL STUDIES	LIFE SKILLS	FINE ARTS
★ Demonstrate understanding of the spatial information of various kinds of maps	★ *Home arts:* Visualize various home care items and produce them (for example, decor for a room, a meal and its presentation)	★ Demonstrate understanding of music nomenclature through visual symbols or colors
★ Demonstrate understanding of the aspects of various current events through mind maps	★ *Driver's education:* Demonstrate knowledge of the signs of the road and the ability to recognize various potentially dangerous driving situations, as well as how to parallel park	★ Design an appropriate setting for a play or story
★ Recognize other cultures through their visual art forms (for example, painting, sculpture)		★ Express musical motifs and emotions through drawing, painting, and sculpture
★ Visualize what your life would be like if you grew up in another culture	★ *Industrial arts:* Design something from a blueprint or make a drawing showing how to make something	★ Demonstrate understanding of a variety of ballroom dance steps by placing cut-out footsteps on the floor
★ Create a current events montage with pictures from magazines and newspapers	★ *Computer science:* Explain keyboard functions through flowcharts or diagrams	★ Recognize, reproduce, and understand the artistic styles of a variety of visual artists
★ Create a photo album or videocassette to demonstrate understanding of another culture	★ *Physical education:* Use visualization and video tapes to improve skill at playing a sport	★ Write an original poem using colors, patterns, designs, and images to enhance its message

Bodily-Kinesthetic Intelligence

Performance-Based Assessment

Performance-based assessment asks students to express their learning and knowledge through practical demonstration or action. The primary mode of this assessment form is physical movement, including physical exercise, sports games, and dramatic enactment.

These tests should require students to use the capacities of bodily-kinesthetic intelligence: control of various motor activities (including voluntary, involuntary, and preprogrammed body movements), the mind and body connection, expanding awareness through the body, improved body functioning, and mimetic abilities.

Students must be able to "em-body" their learning in the language of physical movement, namely, dance, drama, gestures, role-playing, expressive body language, mime, dance, and charades.

Assessment Instruments

- **lab experiments**—being able to perform successfully certain specified processes or experiments
- **dramatization**—enacting various concepts, stages of a process, or events
- **original dance**—choreographing an orchestrated flow of body movements that embody various things being studied
- **charades and mimes**—acting out or role-playing various concepts and ideas from a lesson
- **impersonations**—becoming another person and acting, speaking, feeling, behaving, as that person would in a given situation
- **human tableaux**—using body sculpture to exhibit understanding of a concept or process (for example, arranging a group of people into a "living sculpture"
- **invention projects**—creating various kinds of products with the hands to show understanding and application of learning
- **physical exercise routines and games**—creating movement exercises and games that use various concepts or processes
- **skill demonstrations**—demonstrating understanding of a topic through proficient execution of related activities
- **illustrations through body language and gesture**—making appropriate physical signals and postures to illustrate concepts or ideas one has studied

---

Bodily-Kinesthetic Assessment Ideas

LANGUAGE ARTS	HISTORY	MATHEMATICS	SCIENCE/HEALTH
★ Physically embody different linguistic concepts (for example, the meaning of vocabulary words, spelling words, the function of the parts of speech)	★ Act out various scenes and events from history using charades or human tableaux	★ Act out story problems, embody geometric formulas, or show math operations through physical movement	★ Demonstrate scientific concepts and processes kinesthetically (for example, states of matter, parts or functions of a cell, or genetic displacement)
★ Show knowledge of body language as a way of communicating feelings, thoughts, and ideas in literature	★ Demonstrate understanding of dramatic techniques used in different historical periods	★ Demonstrate understanding of the logic and mathematical patterns of traditional dances	★ Demonstrate healthy versus unhealthy lifestyles or practices
★ Dramatize a modern sequel for something in literature	★ Pretend to be a historical figure dealing with a modern challenge	★ Show kinesthetic understanding of fractions (for example, showing wholes and parts of a group)	★ Successfully perform scientific lab experiments
★ Show understanding of a character in a story or a play through impersonation	★ Perform dances from different periods of history, telling about the period through the dance	★ Create and demonstrate understanding of human graphs (arranging people along a continuum based on feelings or opinions)	★ Make up a physical exercise routine, dance, or game based on a scientific process (for example, states of matter aerobics or photosynthesis basketball)
★ Act out an idea for a creative writing exercise before writing	★ Create a physical "walk through" of various scenes and periods in history	★ Invent something that uses math concepts (for example, a playground)	★ Design a health awareness kitbag for promoting consciousness of healthy practices (for example, diet and exercise)
★ Create language arts–based sports games (for example, grammar baseball, syntax relays, and so on)	★ Design an adventure game based on historical periods and events, then play it	★ Make up a dance based on math processes (for example, finding a common denominator, a square root, counting by 2s)	★ Create a science-based scavenger hunt (for example, find examples of different classifications of living things)

Bodily-Kinesthetic
Assessment Ideas *(continued)*

GLOBAL STUDIES	LIFE SKILLS	FINE ARTS
★ Perform folk dances from different cultures to show understanding of customs, values, lifestyle, and so on	★ *Home arts:* Translate a recipe into a dish or a pattern into a piece of clothing	★ Execute successfully a variety of dance steps and movements
★ Demonstrate recognition of various cultures via physical gestures, body language, or customs	★ *Driver's education:* Demonstrate various kinds of mechanical aspects of driving or caring for a car (for example, changing a tire, checking the oil or tire pressure)	★ Act out a variety of emotional states
★ Simulate or role-play the ways in which different cultures might react to or deal with various problems or challenging situations	★ *Industrial arts:* Operate properly different shop machines to create various products	★ Demonstrate musical concepts and forms with the body (for example, the physical look of Souza marches, Strauss waltzes, or modern rock)
★ Create a kinesthetic legend for a map (for example, show geographical features through physical embodiment)	★ *Computer science:* Perform different computing skills on demand	★ Show the physical equivalents of various artists' styles of creation and artistic expression
★ Show knowledge of cultures via the physical games the people play	★ *Physical education:* Successfully perform various physical exercises or movement routines or mimic movements of a physically educated person	★ Create human tableaux and sculptures that show the meaning of a piece of poetry
★ Plan a cultural or geography field trip that would help someone understand another culture or features of an area		★ Make up an original dance to communicate an idea, belief, opinion, or emotion

Musical-Rhythmic Intelligence

Auditory-Based Assessment

Auditory-based assessment asks students to demonstrate their knowledge and learning through hearing and producing sound. The primary mode of these tests is tonal and rhythmic patterns, including sounds produced with the vocal chords and the body, sounds in the environment (natural and otherwise), sounds from musical and percussion instruments, and sounds produced mechanically.

These tests should require students to use the capacities of musical-rhythmic intelligence: appreciation for the structure of music, awareness of the schema for hearing music, sensitivity to the qualities of various sounds (including pitch, timbre, tempo, and tone), creation and reproduction of melody and rhythm, and expression of thoughts and feelings through tonal, vibrational, and rhythmic patterns.

Students must be able to show understanding by producing meaningful sounds and recognizing a range of sounds and rhythms related to what is being assessed.

Assessment Instruments

- **creating concept songs and raps**—creating songs or raps that demonstrate understanding of certain concepts, ideas, or processes
- **illustrating with sound**—making sounds that are appropriate to and suggestive of certain concepts being studied
- **discerning rhythmic patterns**—recognizing various rhythms, beats, and vibrations related to things one has learned
- **composing music**—creating musical patterns and melody to accompany various processes, concepts, or ideas in a lesson
- **linking music and rhythm with concepts**—relating existing musical-rhythmic compositions to concepts, processes, and ideas being studied
- **orchestrating music**—illustrating understanding of a concept through such things as the timing, volume, and pacing of rhythmic patterns
- **recognizing tonal patterns and quality**—recognizing tonal patterns that are related to specific topics being studied
- **analyzing musical structure**—sensing and explaining connections among various musical forms and certain concepts
- **reproducing musical and rhythmic patterns**—exhibiting understanding through replication of music and rhythm related to specific topics

---

Musical-Rhythmic Assessment Ideas

LANGUAGE ARTS	HISTORY	MATHEMATICS	SCIENCE/HEALTH
★ Associate various kinds of music and rhythm with phases of the writing process, parts of a story, or parts of speech	★ Show recognition of the music forms of different historical periods	★ Demonstrate understanding of numeric patterns through rhythm and beat (for example, regular time, double time, 3/4 time, and so on)	★ Recognize various natural phenomena or animals by the sounds they make
★ Demonstrate understanding of the meters of different kinds of poetry	★ Associate modern songs with historical events and explain the connections noted	★ Create songs or raps to explain various math concepts, processes, or operations	★ Create a symphony of sound accompaniment for various scientific processes (for example, cell division, chemical bonding)
★ Illustrate a story or recount its parts through sound and music	★ Explain key characteristics of a historical period as they are reflected in the music of that period	★ Demonstrate understanding of math principles embodied in musical pieces (for example, different note values, correct number of beats in a measure, and so on)	★ Demonstrate understanding of various healthy body rhythms (for example, heart rate needed for effective cardiovascular exercise, rhythm of healthy eating practices)
★ Write about your understanding of the message in the lyrics of a song	★ Create songs or raps to explain key historical facts and figures		
★ Create new words for an old song to demonstrate rules of grammar, spelling, and so on	★ Show the development and evolution that took place in a historical period as they are reflected in the sounds and tones of that era	★ Make sounds for math operations and processes (this would be like Victor Borge's phonetic punctuation applied to math)	★ Explain what happens in various scientific processes through rhythm and beats (for example, stages of digestion, phases of an earthquake, states of matter)
★ Make up phonetic systems to demonstrate understanding of punctuation, parts of speech, pronunciation of vocabulary words, and so on (a la Victor Borge's phonetic punctuation routine)	★ Show understanding of various musical forms as they relate to historical events (for example, swing and big band during World War II, folk songs during the Vietnam War, and so on)	★ Select appropriate background music for solving math problems	★ Create a science process Broadway musical (for example, *The Phantom of Photosynthesis*)
		★ Create musical games that demonstrate math understanding (for example, guess the pattern of notes in a song)	★ Demonstrate understanding of beats and rhythms that occur in natural cycles (for example, seasons, phases of an earthquake)

Musical-Rhythmic
Assessment Ideas (continued)

GLOBAL STUDIES	LIFE SKILLS	FINE ARTS
★ Recognize the rhythmic patterns and musical expressions and sounds of different cultures	★ *Home arts:* Write a song or rap that demonstrates understanding of the procedures used to make something	★ Represent various kinds of music and rhythm in drawing, painting, or sculpture
★ Incorporate songs, rhythms, and sounds from a variety of cultures in a composition on global understanding	★ *Driver's education:* Demonstrate knowledge of various sounds related to driving and what one should do in different situations related to driving (for example, mechanical trouble, emergency vehicles approaching, different traffic and weather conditions)	★ Create an original dance and perform classical dance steps based on the music (for example, waltz, cha cha, or two step)
★ Demonstrate knowledge of musical instruments from different cultures and the sounds they make (for example, didjereedoo, Peruvian flute, sitar)		★ Compose a musical or rhythmic piece to express various feelings, emotions, or ideas
★ Create a sound-based legend for a map (that is, showing understanding of geography through sounds)	★ *Industrial arts:* Demonstrate recognition of the sounds different machines make and troubleshoot problems with the machines based on the sounds	★ Show recognition of various rhythms, instruments, and techniques used in music
★ Make and play instruments people in other cultures use	★ *Computer science:* Explain various computer processes or signals using the sounds the computer makes; use music and rhythms to increase skill (for example, entering data more quickly)	★ Turn a nonmusical drama into a musical by integrating music at appropriate places
★ Explain different perspectives of current affairs through lyrics of contemporary songs		★ Enhance the impact of an original poem's message with music or rhythmic accompaniment
	★ *Physical education:* Recognize different sports via sound and rhythmic patterns, or use music and rhythms to increase skill or performance (for example, dribbling a ball)	

Interpersonal Intelligence

Relational-Based Assessment

Relational-based assessment asks students to demonstrate their knowledge and learning as part of a group or cooperative effort. The primary mode of this assessment is meaningful person-to-person relating and effective teamwork, including such things as reflective listening, trust of teammates, encouragement and support of others, division of labor, empathy, building consensus, and transcending self-interest for the sake of the team.

These tests should require students to use the capacities of interpersonal intelligence: verbal and nonverbal communication skills; sensitivity to others' moods, motives, and feelings; cooperation within a group; empathy with other people; discernment of another's underlying intentions and perspectives based on behavior; and creation and maintenance of synergy (*synergy* comes from the Greek *syn ergos,* which means "a spontaneous working together").

Students must be able to show their individual learning and knowledge by helping the team succeed.

Assessment Instruments

- **group "jigsaws"**—taking an examination as a team with each member doing a part of the test
- **explaining to or teaching another**—telling another person the answer to a question on a test and convincing that person that the answer is correct
- **"think-pair-share"**—telling answers to another, who in turn tells another, and so on
- **"round robin"**—doing a part of the test, then passing it on for others to build on the work
- **giving and receiving feedback**—evaluating team members' responses to examination questions, then coaching one another to come up with better answers
- **interviews, questionnaires, and "people searches"**—getting answers from one another for questions on a test and knowing if the answers are correct
- **empathic processing**—demonstrating understanding of a partner's answer to a question and why the answer is correct or incorrect
- **random group quizzes**—studying certain ideas as a team, then answering questions about material as the teacher randomly chooses group members
- **assess your teammates**—making up tests for one another, administering the tests, and checking the answers for understanding
- **test, coach, and retest**—discussing the questions missed on a test and helping one another to understand mistakes, then retaking the test

---

Interpersonal Assessment Ideas

LANGUAGE ARTS	HISTORY	MATHEMATICS	SCIENCE/HEALTH
★ With a partner, create a story that has no ending, then tell it to another pair who will create the ending	★ Stand in the shoes of someone from the past and discuss a modern issue (for example, what might Harriet Tubman say about current racial issues, or what would Thomas Jefferson say about our treatment of the environment?)	★ Solve mathematical problems in a round-robin fashion (that is, each person on a team does part of the problem then passes it on)	★ Interview a scientific process as if it were a guest on a talk show (for example, ask the digestive process to explain how it works)
★ Listen to a speech, then summarize or paraphrase what was said		★ Create a problem and find someone who can solve it	★ Do "jigsaw" lab experiments (that is, each team member draws from a hat a part of the experiment and performs that part)
★ Hold mock trials of various villains from literature	★ Explain how history might have been different if certain events had not happened (for example, the American colonies had not been taxed without representation)	★ Assign math-process roles in cooperative groups (for example, assign one student to be the multiplier, another to be the divider, another to be the adder, and so on)	★ Organize a team to perform a scientific experiment, including assignment of roles, steps, reporting of results, and drawing conclusions
★ Play a particular role in a story and tell what you would do and how the story would be different if you were in it			
★ Do "round robin" creative writing exercises (that is, each person starts writing and passes the work to others to complete)	★ Take both sides in a debate about a historical issue	★ Teach a partner how to solve a problem, then test the partner and help him or her be successful	★ With a group, brainstorm guidelines to healthy living and reach a consensus on the most important ones
★ Evaluate and improve each other's written work	★ Justify the actions of certain historical figures within the context of their times	★ Brainstorm approaches to solving a complex or ambiguous problem, then try each approach and evaluate it	★ With a team, create and perform a play for conducting an experiment that applies the scientific method
	★ Create various "If I had been there I would have . . . " scenarios	★ Correct one another's answers to problems on a test and coach one another to correct wrong answers	
	★ Design group research projects that apply learnings from the past to contemporary issues		

Multiple Intelligence Approaches to Assessment © 1994 Zephyr Press, Tucson, Arizona

Interpersonal
Assessment Ideas (continued)

GLOBAL STUDIES	LIFE SKILLS	FINE ARTS

★ Organize and conduct a health survey, summarize the results, and report the results to others

★ Demonstrate an understanding of how someone from another culture might solve a problem in our culture

★ Show empathy for and understanding of both sides in a current affairs debate (for example, pro-life/pro-choice)

★ Make up a survey to gain multiple perspectives on a current affair

★ Interview people of different cultural backgrounds and present the results

★ Use a map to explain to a partner how to get someplace; see if the partner can get there by following your instructions

★ Set up a group problem-solving session to address an environmental issue

★ *Home arts:* Demonstrate ability to perform various tasks chosen by the class (for example, make a specified dish or piece of clothing)

★ *Driver's education:* Evaluate one another on driving skills and capacities (for example, simulate the state driving test)

★ *Industrial arts:* Hold a class or team discussion or evaluation of a product in which you include suggestions for improvement

★ *Computer science:* Each team or class member teaches another something learned about the computer (for example, a shortcut, how to customize a program)

★ *Physical education:* Show knowledge and skill in executing responsibilities of various positions in team sports

★ Demonstrate ability to blend individual performance skills with a team (for example, dance steps, musical ensemble)

★ Create a mural with each team member demonstrating an art concept in the mural

★ Based on understanding of a character, predict what will happen next in a drama

★ Compose a musical piece that incorporates various musical skills and techniques suggested by a team

★ Create a dance or drama to show effective teamwork (for example, conflict resolution, building consensus)

★ Write a poem with a team to express team members' various perspectives or feelings about something

Intrapersonal Intelligence

Psychological-Based Assessment

Psychological-based assessment asks students to demonstrate their knowledge and learning through expression of what they feel about the material and how it may have informed or changed their self-understanding, personal philosophy, beliefs, or values.

These tests should require students to use the capacities of intrapersonal intelligence: concentration of the mind, mindfulness ("stop and smell the roses" activities), metacognitive processing (thinking about and analyzing one's own patterns of thinking), awareness of and expression of different feelings, transpersonal sense of the self ("no one is an island"), and higher-order thinking and reasoning (for example, Bloom's taxonomy).

Students must be able to show their knowledge of a given subject in and through introspection about the topics, such as through reflective writing and speaking, symbolic representations of meaning and understanding, or applications of ideas beyond the classroom.

Assessment Instruments

- **autobiographical reporting**—writing a report on ways that a concept or idea has informed or had an impact on one's self-understanding

- **personal application scenarios**—telling ways that one could apply or use certain information or concepts in the task of daily living

- **metacognitive surveys and questionnaires**—relating how one approached particular problems and evaluating the strategies used

- **higher-order questions and answers**—recalling facts, then moving to applying the process and synthesizing dimensions of something being studied

- **concentration tests**—choosing something from a list of options on which to focus that can be used to demonstrate understanding and knowledge of a topic

- **feelings diaries and logs**—writing about personal feelings or emotional responses to different subjects being studied

- **personal projection**—expressing "If I were . . . I would . . ." about persons, characters, or situations being studied.

- **self-identification reporting**—telling about personal likes and dislikes and what persons or situations were identified with

- **personal history correlation**—finding correlative patterns between own life and subjects being studied

- **personal priorities and goals**—reporting on how a subject being studied affected sense of priorities in life

---

Intrapersonal Assessment Ideas

LANGUAGE ARTS	HISTORY	MATHEMATICS	SCIENCE/HEALTH
★ Demonstrate comprehension of a story by becoming a character in it and telling what you would have done or how you would have acted	★ Reflect on how your life would be different if certain historical events had turned out differently; include your feelings about the difference	★ Demonstrate knowledge of math concepts by telling how you can use them to enhance your life beyond school	★ Demonstrate understanding of health concepts by designing a personal health and wellness plan (for example, diet, exercise, sleep)
★ Demonstrate different poetic forms by writing about something important to you	★ Demonstrate understanding of historical topics by telling how and why you personally identify with certain historical figures	★ Analyze personal statistics using various math concepts and operations (for example, the ratio of shoe size to height, square root of your weight)	★ Demonstrate knowledge of various scientific processes by reflecting on the most exciting and interesting parts for you
★ Illustrate understanding of characters in a play or story by telling what you like and dislike about each	★ Draw analogies between your life and historical events (for example, your struggle for independence)	★ Assess your problem-solving skills and make a personal plan to improve them	★ Write journal entries in which you talk with different parts of the body, scientific processes, and so on
★ List questions about your own life that a piece of literature has raised	★ Compare and contrast your personal philosophy with those of people from the past	★ Explain your intuitions about an answer to a problem, then solve the problem and reflect on your intuitive response	★ Describe how you feel about each phase of a scientific process or about various health facts
★ Write a brief story in which you are the hero	★ Explain why and how studying a particular historical period can help us address or inform us about a contemporary issue	★ Recognize the relationships between personal life problems and math patterns (for example, creating a budget to save money for something you want to buy)	★ Create a self-directed learning experiment in which you apply science and health to an area of personal interest
★ Tell how reading a certain story or piece of poetry has changed or amplified your self-understanding	★ Choose a problem or challenge you are facing and create an imaginary conversation between yourself and a historic figure based on that problem	★ Explore a personal problem or challenge through math (for example, graph and track your improvement in dealing with siblings, parents, or difficult peers)	★ Show the roles various patterns of nature and science play in your life (for example, seasonal changes, digestive system)

Intrapersonal
Assessment Ideas *(continued)*

GLOBAL STUDIES	LIFE SKILLS	FINE ARTS
★ Reflect on changes in your self-understanding due to encounters with other cultures	★ *Home arts:* Make something, such as a dish or a piece of clothing, changing the directions to reflect your personal tastes	★ Use different art forms to express personal feelings about various topics
★ Describe your feelings about cultures whose ideas differ from your own (for example food, family life, dress, religious customs)	★ *Driver's education:* Write about things you need to do to remind yourself to drive defensively	★ Demonstrate understanding of various musical forms by analyzing the feelings they evoke in you
★ Share your own opinions and feelings about issues in the news	★ *Industrial arts:* Create and carry out a plan to make something you want	★ Use a variety of dance forms to create an original dance about something that concerns you
★ Write an autobiography as if you'd been born in another culture	★ *Computer science:* Create five applications of computer technology that will enhance your daily life	★ Assess your performance of a piece of music, a dramatic enactment, or your creation of an art form (painting, drawing, sculpture, poetry)
★ List your personal agenda for achieving cross-cultural understanding	★ *Physical education:* Evaluate your performance of various physical education skills, including strategies for improvement	★ Create a play for integrating art, dance, music, sculpture, poetry, and drama into your daily life
★ Choose different areas of the world on a map and explain the positive and negative aspects of living in each		★ Create a piece of art to explain your values, philosophy, and beliefs

Using the Multiple Intelligence Assessment Instruments Menu to Design Tests

An important cautionary point to keep in mind when designing the kinds of performance assessments I have suggested in this chapter is that you could have inauthentic performances and performances that are *not* intelligence based or intelligence fair. Carol Meyers (1992) helps define the criteria of performance authenticity:

> Performance assessment and authentic assessment are often used interchangeably, but do they mean the same thing? Although both labels might appropriately apply to some types of assessment, they are not synonymous. . . .
>
> Performance assessment refers to the kind of student response to be examined; authentic assessment refers to the context in which that response is performed. Although not all performance assessments are authentic, it is difficult to imagine an authentic assessment that would not also be a performance assessment. . . .
>
> In a performance assessment, the student completes or demonstrates the same behavior that the assessor desires to measure. . . .
>
> In an authentic assessment, the student not only completes or demonstrates the desired behavior, but also does it in a real-life context. (39–40)

Following are several suggestions for using the Multiple Intelligence Assessment Instruments Menu presented earlier. I make these suggestions so you can supplement, enhance, intensify, and deepen your instruction; I do not intend them to be used in isolation from a full-blown multiple intelligence approach to teaching and learning. As you by now understand from reading this book, my major presupposition about assessment is that it should be one with instruction and that it is the tool *par excellence* that we have at our disposal to amplify the deep learning, knowing, and understanding of our students.

Behind these processes is the assumption that you have thoroughly taught your students *about* the multiple intelligences and that teaching *with* multiple intelligences is central to your instructional practice. (See *Seven Pathways of Learning: Teaching Students and Parents about Multiple Intelligences* and *Seven Ways of Teaching: The Artistry of Teaching with Multiple Intelligences* for additional resources.)

PROCESS 1: 7-IN-1 TESTS

Clearly define your objectives for a given testing period, including knowledge and understanding of academic content and process. Select one instrument from each intelligence area that you feel will help students show you what they know. Design the test so that students will use all the instruments you have selected.

You can vary this test by explaining your objectives to your students and asking them to select from the menu seven different ways or techniques they would like to use to demonstrate their understanding.

When to Use 7-in-1 Tests

You can use this process most effectively when you want to be sure that students have really understood something. Just because students can write a convincing essay or can choose the right items on a multiple choices test does not mean they truly understand.

PROCESS 2: 7 OPTIONS

Again, make sure your testing objectives are clear to you and to your students. Then, using the Instruments Menu, choose one assessment instrument from each intelligence that would be an acceptable way for students to demonstrate their knowledge. Carefully explain each test to students, including what is required and how the test will be scored. Then allow students to choose a test they feel they can use to demonstrate most fully their knowledge and understanding.

You can vary this test by having students individually create tests for themselves that would prove to you that they have mastered the material. They would first choose an instrument from the menu and then submit a plan for their test for your approval. Remember the responsibility is theirs to show their understanding through the instrument they choose.

When to Use 7 Options

You can use this process most effectively when you want to maximize the success quotient for all students and to read between the lines of their knowing and understanding to discern areas about which they might be confused, where they lack understanding, have blind spots, and need reteaching in a different way.

PROCESS 3: INTELLIGENCE FOCUS

Choose an instrument from a particular intelligence that is in line with your testing objectives and design a test that asks students to demonstrate their knowledge and understanding in and through a predetermined intelligence. The key is to make sure that the test is intelligence fair; that is, it occurs within the language, symbol system, and mode of the intelligence you have chosen.

A second option would be to design a test that emphasizes the unique manifestations of the intelligences within a particular subject area or discipline, for example, the dances of a historical era, the rhythmic patterns of a scientific process, the visual art of a culture, or the logic of a math problem challenge.

When to Use Intelligence Focus

You can use this process most effectively when you are concerned with the transfer of learning from a particular discipline or subject area to other areas of the curriculum or to an understanding of everyday applications of knowledge in the so-called real world.

PROCESS 4: RANDOM DRAWING

From the menu, select two or three assessment instruments for each intelligence that align with your objectives. Couch the knowledge to be tested in the unique language or mode of the instrument: "Create a sculpture out of clay that shows . . . " "Write a poem or limerick that shows . . . " or "Make up a dance routine to show . . . " Write these items on slips of paper, put the slips in a hat, and have students select their tests.

When to Use Random Drawing

You can use this process most effectively when you want to promote creative thinking about what you have been teaching and when you are interested in challenging students to make unusual or less obvious connections among a specific body of knowledge and other areas of the curriculum and life beyond the school.

Multiple Intelligence Approaches to Assessment © 1994 Zephyr Press, Tucson, Arizona

PROCESS 5: PARTNERS TESTING PARTNERS

Present to the class your objectives for a particular test. Assign each student a partner. Each pair selects from the Instruments Menu two instruments, one for each partner, that they believe are most appropriate to help them demonstrate individually the given objectives. Partners then create the tests *for each other* in the mode of the selected intelligence and instrument. The partners agree on how the product will be scored. After preparing the test, each partner will administer his or her test to the other.

When to Use Partners Testing Partners

You can use this process most effectively when students have a great deal of skill in cooperative and collaborative learning and when you feel that they will benefit from teaching and learning from each other. You can also use it when you want to increase your students' sense of responsibility for their own and each other's learning.

Scoring Multiperceptual Tests

The key supposition underlying the following suggestions is the same as that underlying the entire book; namely, all assessment should benefit students by enhancing, deepening, and expanding their learning. A second assumption is that in order to be fair to students, we should use a variety of scoring models. Scoring to reflect the many facets of the students' abilities rather than giving a single aggregate score will ensure that all aspects of students' performances have been thoroughly evaluated.

To implement any of the following models will require extensive public discussion and a consensus-building involving professional educators (teachers, principals, and district-level administrators), experts in various academic disciplines beyond formal education, those who set national and state educational policy (legislators and school board members), parents, those who determine college entrance requirements, members of the business community or other potential future employers, and other concerned members of society. These approaches to scoring assume that to gain a holistic picture of students' learning, no single test or scoring mechanism will suffice.

Multiple Intelligence Approaches to Assessment © 1994 Zephyr Press, Tucson, Arizona

Levels of Mastery Scoring

The following model is based on Connecticut's performance criteria for assessing performance in foreign languages (see Wiggins 1988). The model suggests scoring students in a particular discipline as if they were apprentices learning a craft or skill. An evaluation would be similar to what they might receive if they were being evaluated by a master craftsman or, in this case, the master (the teacher) of the discipline. You must define carefully the specific expectations and criteria by which you will assess students for each level in each academic discipline you will be assessing. Students' work could be scored using categories such as these, and the students could use the assessments to improve their performances and to help them set realistic and fair goals for themselves.

☆ **NOVICE LEVEL**

Students at this level demonstrate the ability to recall basic information such as facts, figures, and dates they have learned.

☆ **INTERMEDIATE LEVEL (basic)**

Students at this level demonstrate an explicit understanding of the meanings of information they have learned and a simple, direct application of their knowledge within the context of the original learning.

☆ **INTERMEDIATE LEVEL (complex)**

Students at this level demonstrate a creative, inferential, and process understanding of the information they have learned that goes beyond the context of the original learning; in other words, they demonstrate that they can transfer the learning to other subjects in the curriculum.

☆ **ADVANCED LEVEL**

Students at this level demonstrate a genuine mastery of knowledge that goes beyond the structures of formal education, including understanding the import and implications of what they have learned, its practical application in their lives outside of school, and a general integration and transfer of learning.

Assessor and Assessee Interaction Scoring

Grant Wiggins (1988) also describes the basic process of a model based on the British Assessment of Performance Units (APUs), which assumes an active interaction between the assessor and assessee: "The assessor is meant to probe, prompt, and even teach, if necessary, to be sure of the student's ability and to 'enable' the learner to learn from the assessment" (17). This model reveals the relative levels of students' achievement and *how they did it*.

Successful Responses

No help or coaching required:

★ **Student is successful with no help from the assessor**—student is able to demonstrate understanding without any help from the assessor.

★ **Student successfully corrects an unsuccessful response without help from the assessor**—student's first response is unsuccessful, but he or she corrects the response with no prompting from the assessor.

Help or coaching provided:

★ **Student is successful with some coaching from the assessor**—student may receive different scores based on the different degrees of assistance he or she required (for example, the student would receive a higher score for an area in which he or she needed only one cue and would receive a lower score for an area in which he or she needed four cues).

★ **Student is successful, but only after direct reteaching by the assessor**—the coaching of the previous level did not produce a successful response; the assessor had to go over related concepts again and then the student could produce a successful response

Unsuccessful Responses

Help and coaching provided:

★ **Student is unsuccessful despite coaching and direct teaching**—student could not produce the appropriate response even with direct help.

No help or coaching provided:

★ **Student is unsuccessful and assessor did not prompt or teach**—student is not successful and assessor did not attempt to help the student deliver an appropriate response.

You would have to define clearly each phase of the assessment interaction process so that students understand the scores for the different levels and what constitutes a lack of success. This approach offers at least three major benefits to assessment. First, it provides a number of ways for all students to succeed. Second, an assessment instrument that is scored in this fashion will itself be an authentic learning experience, for students have an opportunity and are expected to interact with the assessor, asking questions if they are not clear about what is being asked, explaining and elaborating their responses if necessary, and defending their answers to convince the assessor they have mastered the required materials, skills, and so on. Finally, this approach gives students a fair way to improve their assessed performance.

Degree of Difficulty Scoring

This approach to scoring is often called "graduated criteria scoring" and bears some similarities to the "levels of mastery scoring" model. The degree of difficulty model is based roughly on the philosophy of the British GSCE exams and the competency-based testing at Alverno College in Milwaukee, Wisconsin (see Wiggins 1988). The model makes the following assumptions:

- Not all students must be tested in the same way, at the same level, at the same time.

- Students should be given some choice about *when* they are ready to be tested.

- Students should be given some choice about the *level of difficulty* at which they feel confident to be tested.

- Students should be given options on *how* they want to be tested (that is, the testing instruments used).

- There are multiple levels and dimensions to success in any discipline, including such things as content mastery, process comprehension, skill demonstration, and transfer of understanding.

Each level of difficulty builds on and encompasses all previous levels.

LEVEL 1: SIMPLE 1 (focus on information recall)

This level involves being able to recall and reproduce information studied in a text or gained from a lecture. The form of these kinds of tests is usually multiple choice, fill in the blanks, matching, true and false, and so on.

LEVEL 2: SIMPLE 2 (focus on execution of process and operation)

This level involves being able to recall and duplicate the performance of standard processes and operations of a discipline (for example, finding a square root or putting verbs in proper tense). These tests usually ask students to show they know how to use given processes or operations.

Multiple Intelligence Approaches to Assessment © 1994 Zephyr Press, Tucson, Arizona

LEVEL 3: COMPLEX (focus on problem-solving competency)

This level involves using the previous two levels to solve a prescribed problem or deal with a challenge that would require using the information and processes being tested. The form of these tests can vary widely depending on what is being tested (for example, an essay in literature or history, a complicated math problem involving a number of steps, or a formal lab experiment in science).

LEVEL 4: ADVANCED (focus on complicated applications)

This level involves the performance of tasks and the solving of problems that are typical or representative of the particular discipline being tested. For example, a test in social studies might ask students to demonstrate real understanding of and empathy for other cultures, or in writing, students might be asked to produce different types of essays, poetry, and so on, on a single topic.

LEVEL 5: VOCATIONAL AND AVOCATIONAL (focus on transfer, synthesis, and integration)

This level involves the real-world application and use of the knowledge, skills, competencies, processes, and so on, of a particular discipline. The form of these tests tends to be open-ended. These are often simulation exams that represent problems from the workplace or one's personal life in which an intimate, integrated application of one's knowledge and understanding is required.

There could be five separate tests, or within one test there could be a set of graduated subquestions under the main problem to be solved. Students could select the level to answer, with more points being given for the more difficult questions. The major value of this approach is that it points students in the right direction and gives us a way to help them set clear, realizable, and individually appropriate goals for their schooling. Students should be allowed to choose the level of difficulty at which they believe they can demonstrate successfully their learning and to challenge themselves to new heights. They should not be penalized if they attempt a more difficult test or level of questions than they can handle. We must also get used to the idea that not all students will want to, nor do they all need to be able to, perform at level 5. At whatever level they perform, however, it should be a challenging and exciting learning experience, and we should use it to help them attain mastery at that level.

The models discussed are only beginning suggestions of new scoring and grading practices. Many others could be suggested as well. For example, we could invent a practice that might be called "cognitive patterns scoring" through which we could observe students' thinking patterns and help them develop fruitful habits of mind. There could be a practice called "self-evaluation scoring" in which students grade themselves on such things as their individual goals or how their self-concept and self-understanding have changed or been reinforced by what they have learned in different subjects. There could be a practice called "before, during, and after continuum scoring," which would give a picture of students' journeys throughout the year. The continuum could highlight such things as the growth and development of different skills, competencies, knowledge, and understanding.

The goal of all these models is to help us assess what is happening to students in their education so that we can serve more effectively our students' educational needs. Obviously, we must enlist the professional help of those trained in the areas of psychometrics, statistics, and testing to help construct a test scoring and grading system that, first of all, genuinely benefits students at the point of enhancing, deepening, and expanding their learning. Second, this new system must be a fair and accurate measure of what students are actually learning in our schools and how effectively we are reaching our students.

Multiple Intelligence Approaches to Assessment © 1994 Zephyr Press, Tucson, Arizona

7

Classroom-Based Informal Assessment

Practices for Ongoing Evaluation of Students

Assessing learning in natural contexts, in familiar environments, and with familiar tools and activities enables students to demonstrate their knowledge more effectively than through decontextualized, standardized approaches. The boundaries between assessment and instruction begin to dissolve when assessment occurs while students are actively engaged in usual classroom experiences.

—Campbell, Dickinson, and Campbell

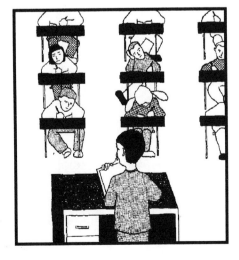

In addition to the formal testing instruments suggested in chapter 6, I also advocate several supplementary, informal models to help us create multimodal approaches to the assessment of students' academic progress on a daily basis. Each model is designed to help students give us an overall picture of their knowledge and skills. Each asks students to move from passive to active learning. Each assumes that students are responsible for their own learning. Together these models provide students with many options to be successful, as they become our partners in demonstrating and celebrating academic excellence.

Student Portfolios

Portfolio assessment provides a variety of means to document and assess students' work. A student portfolio is similar to the portfolio an artist or photographer carries to show prospective clients examples of his or her best work. For assessment purposes, students maintain collections of their best work—work that demonstrates their academic progress, skill development, and human growth and development. A portfolio is a highly personalized approach to assessment and, as such, creates a perfect structure for both individualized learning and continued work on intelligence development in and through the academic curriculum. In *The Portfolio Approach to Assessment,* Emily Grady (1992) observes,

> The most obvious benefit of this type of assessment is that most of the contents of the portfolio are *actual pieces of student work, not approximations supplied by a score on a standardized test. . . .*
>
> The portfolio represents a range of efforts and tangible achievements; it presents a learning history. In a well-designed portfolio system, the student selects the pieces of work to be included in the portfolio. The student has the chance to revise it, perfect it, evaluate it, and explain it. It is different from work completed just to fulfill an assignment or written only for the teacher's eyes; a piece created for the portfolio bears a piece of the student's identity. . . . It represents the student in a concrete and authentic way that a stanine score cannot do. (12; emphasis mine)

This approach to assessment matches assessment in the "real world." That is, we produce something (a written report for the boss, a proposal for a client, an actual physical product or invention, a drawing or blueprint, and so on), it is assessed, revisions are made based on the assessment, it is assessed again, and then a final product is created. Portfolio assessment makes assessment an integral part of the learning process. Grady also says, "Performance-based assessment lets students and teachers know exactly what needs exist. Students receive immediate feedback, gain confidence by acknowledgments of their strengths, and gain insight into how to improve. And teacher's professional skills in direct observation and evaluation are emphasized in a way that is missing from test-driven curricula" (13).

On page 154 is a model to help you get started in using portfolios in your classroom. Remember, human beings don't learn and acquire knowledge in a neat and orderly fashion. Allow student portfolios to reflect this haphazardness as well as the excitement of learning, the joy of discovery!

Data for portfolios could literally include anything that will help give you and your students a broad picture of their learning journey during a term or a year. Additional portfolio data could result from teacher observations of students involved in a wide range of activities and learning tasks. Portfolios might even include students' intelligence profiles (see chapter 2). Students could be asked to evaluate themselves regularly in terms of what they have learned, their contributions to the class, their performances on various class-related tasks, their efforts, and so on. Have students create questionnaires and conduct surveys related to classroom topics or themes, or have them report on interviews with other people. Consider asking parents to create a "home report card" in which they tell you (and the student) about their child's development on many different levels, such as what she or he does as hobbies, how she or he relates to siblings, what she or he likes to watch on TV, what she or he reads for fun, what she or he shares from school, and so on. Ask students to be present for parent-teacher conferences and have them conference with their parents about their portfolios.

A Model for Creating Student Portfolios*

> **Q: What should be included to show what students really know?**
>
> **A: Ask the students. Let them help decide.**

Anything they want for whatever reason

Peer observations and evaluations

Evidence of progress toward year's goal

Evidence of self-reflection, self-knowledge, and self-evaluation

Items that indicate transfer of learning (beyond the classroom into life)

STUDENT PORTFOLIO

Items that tell the story of the journey of the year

Information from parents' "home report cards"

Teacher observations, including intelligence profiles

Things that convey learning activities (explicit and implicit artifacts from lessons)

Items that demonstrate "My best work done to date"

Things that show growth and change (skills, interests, extracurricular activities, attitudes)

• Adapted from Lazear, David. *Seven Ways of Teaching: The Artistry of Teaching with Multiple Intelligences.* Palatine, Ill.; Skylight, 1991.

Metacognitive "Process-folios"

Metacognition (thinking about thinking) may be the single most important factor in creating lifelong learners out of our students. Metacognitive processing involves helping students become aware of various patterns of thinking employed in a lesson, helping them evaluate their own and each other's thinking, suporting their ability to improve and alter their thinking processes, and allowing them to select the cognitive strategies and skills they believe will aid in a problem-solving task.

Art Costa (1991) describes metacognition as follows:

> Metacognition is our ability to know what we know and what we don't know. It is our ability to plan a strategy for producing what information is needed, to be conscious of our own steps and strategies during the act of problem solving, and to reflect on and evaluate the productiveness of our own thinking. . . .
>
> We can determine if students are becoming more aware of their own thinking as they are able to describe what goes on in their head when they are thinking. When asked, they can list the steps and tell where they are in the sequence of a problem-solving strategy. They can trace the pathways and dead ends they took on the road to a problem solution. They can describe what data are lacking and their plans for producing those data. (87, 93)

When metacognitive processing is used as an aid to academic assessment, you must find ways to eavesdrop on students in the act of talking to themselves or thinking out loud. If you "listen between the lines" of their reflections on their own thinking about a lesson, their self-evaluations of how they feel they did, their awareness of various thought processes used, and their ideas on improving their thinking and performance, you will be able to assess their understanding of the content of a lesson.

The process-folio is an idea I have borrowed from Howard Gardner. Process-folios go beyond portfolios, which tend to focus on final products. The process-folio also includes the various processes involved in the act of creation. Gardner (1991) describes the process-folio as follows:

> Process-folios represent an effort to capture the steps and phases through which students pass in the course of developing a project, product, or work of art. A complete student process-folio contains initial brainstorming ideas, early drafts, and first critiques; journal entries on "pivotal moments" when ideas gelled; collections of works by others that proved influential or suggestive, in a positive or a negative sense; interim and final drafts; self-critiques by peers, informed mentors, and again, outside experts; and finally some suggestion of how one might build upon the current project in future endeavors. (240)

Following is a beginning model for creating process-folios with your students. Structure the process-folio so that it moves through the different levels of the objective, affective, cognitive, process, metacognitive, and application processes. The levels I suggest in this model are loosely based on Bloom's taxonomy and on Guilford's structure of the intellect. After a lesson, lead students in a group discussion and individual reflection about the lesson and the various learning processes they used.

Remember to listen carefully to what students say and don't say and to what they record and don't record. There are no right answers, but as students share their thoughts and reflections on the process of the lesson, you will have many opportunities to assess their learning and to discover new ways to help them improve, expand, and deepen their learning.

A Model for Metacognitive Process-folios

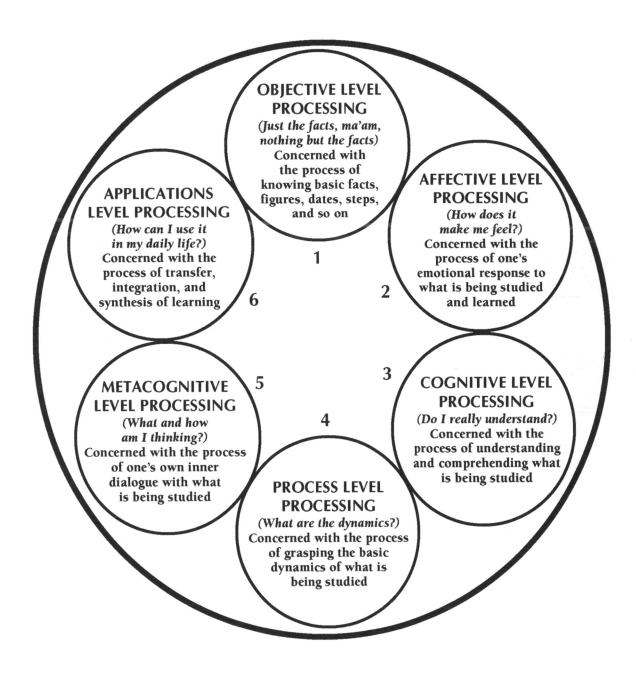

Personal Reflective Journals and Logs

As far as we know, human beings are the only creatures who have the ability to be self-reflective. That is, we possess self-consciousness: the unique capacity to step back from ourselves and watch ourselves involved in any activity. And, what is more, we can alter our behavior even in the midst of it.

This self-reflective or self-awareness dynamic is at the heart of the learning process. It is key to helping students grasp the personal implications of what they are studying. Most of what we learn at deep levels has meaning for us personally. We can learn an immense amount about students' understanding of various concepts if we read between the lines or listen between the words of their personal reflections on the meanings and interpretations they give to what they have learned.

One of the best ways to provide yourself with the opportunity to read between the lines is to encourage students to keep reflective journals or logs to help them be aware of their thoughts, feelings, learnings, questions, and ideas. In *Patterns for Thinking, Patterns for Transfer,* Jim Bellanca and Robin Fogarty (1987) describe the possibilities inherent in thinking logs:

> Writing in the thinking log may take many forms. It may be a narrative, a quote, an essay, jotting, a drawing, a cartoon, a diagram, webs or clusters, a soliloquy, a riddle, a joke, doodles, an opinion, a rebuttal, a dialogue, a letter, a flowchart, or just an assortment of phrases and ideas.
>
> The entries may be reflective, evaluative, questioning, personal, abstract, introspective, cynical, incomplete, revealing, humorous, communicative, thoughtful, poetic, rambling, formative, philosophical, or none of the above. There are no right or wrong answers to do the log. It's just a log of one's thinking—whatever that thinking may be. It's a personal record of the connections being made within the framework of the student's cognitive capacities and their experiences. (226–27)

Following are five models for creating student journals and logs that I suggested in *Seven Ways of Teaching* (Lazear 1991). I have also included an experimental personal reflection log adapted from one in *Seven Ways of Knowing* (Lazear 1991) that suggests a multimodal journaling and logging process. Each model asks students to reflect on the import of a lesson in a particular way. Journals can involve a variety of modes of reflecting, including writing, drawing, painting, sculpting, role-playing, and dancing. As an assessment tool, journals and logs can help us discern the personal impact of lessons on students, and through students' reflections we can often grasp the relative depth and accuracy of their understanding of what we have been teaching.

Models for Student Journals

1. "THINKING LOGS"* *(to process lesson content)*

The main thing I'll remember is . . .

A new insight or discovery is . . .

I really understood . . .

I'm really confused about . . .

Something I can use beyond school is . . .

Connections I'm making with other things I know are . . .

2. BEFORE-AND-AFTER SCENARIOS* *(to process the impact of a lesson)*

Analyze the impact of a unit or lesson on yourself using this chart.

	BEFORE THE UNIT OR LESSON	AFTER THE UNIT OR LESSON
Feelings about it		
Thoughts about it		
Associations with it		
Images or pictures in mind		

Now write "How I'm different as a result of this unit or lesson."

* These models are adapted from Lazear, David. *Seven Ways of Teaching: The Artistry of Teaching with Multiple Intelligences.* Palatine, Ill.: Skylight, 1991.

Models for Student Journals

3. SNAPSHOTS OF THE PAST AND PRESENT* *(to process the import of a lesson)*

Write what you think is the main idea of the lesson.

Pretend this idea had never been thought of. How would life have been different in the past? (Think of 3 ways.)

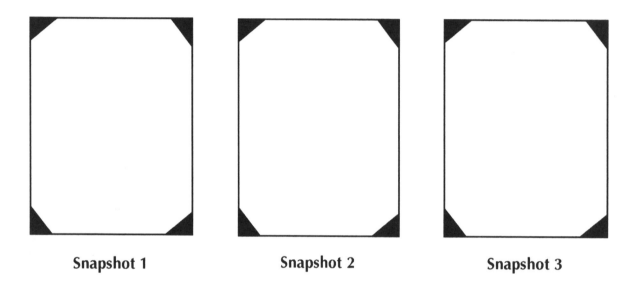

| Snapshot 1 | Snapshot 2 | Snapshot 3 |

How would life be different today without this idea? (Think of 3 ways.)

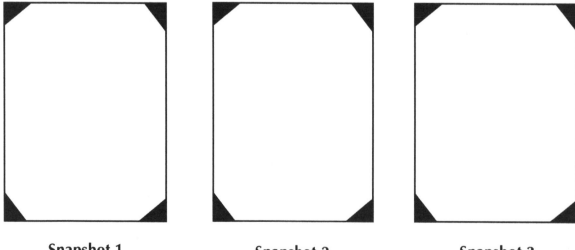

| Snapshot 1 | Snapshot 2 | Snapshot 3 |

* This model is adapted from Lazear, David. *Seven Ways of Teaching: The Artistry of Teaching with Multiple Intelligences*. Palatine, Ill.: Skylight, 1991.

Models for Student Journals

4. CHART YOUR MOODS* *(to process feelings about a day or period)*

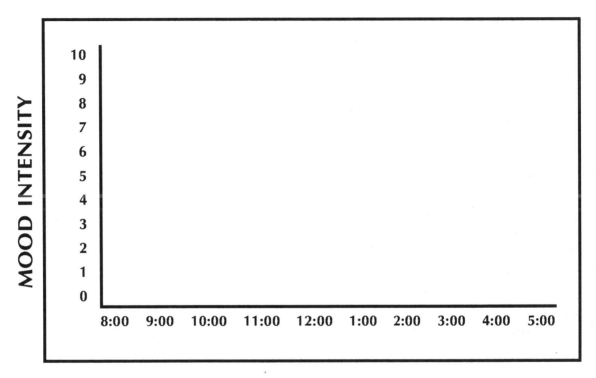

TIME SEQUENCE

1. At the end of the day plot your moods of the day on the graph. (The vertical numbers represent mood intensity and horizontal numbers represent the time sequence.)
2. Place a mark at the high point of the day and one at the low point. Then look at the time before and after these points. Think about other changes in mood. Make marks at the appropriate places.
3. Now connect the marks with a continuous curving line so that you have a visual picture of the mood changes and the "affective flow" of the day.
4. For each point that you have marked along the axes, jot a brief note about what was going on that catalyzed the mood shift.
5. Using colored markers or crayons, create a spectrum of colors from left to right to match the different moods of the day. Note these on the graph.
6. Finally, think of the kind of music you would play as a background for each of the different moods of the day. Note these on the graph.
7. Try doing this every day for a week. At the end of the week lay all of your mood graphs side by side and reflect on the week. What do you learn about yourself as you look at the week in this way?

* This model is adapted from Lazear, David. *Seven Ways of Teaching: The Artistry of Teaching with Multiple Intelligences.* Palatine, Ill.: Skylight, 1991.

Models for Student Journals

5. STEPPING STONES OF THE FUTURE* *(to project future applications of a lesson)*

Write the main idea of the lesson for you

Brainstorm five ways this idea has been or is being applied in our times.

1.

2.

3.

4.

5.

Pretend you can step into the next century. How will this idea be applied then?

---

* This model is adapted from Lazear, David. *Seven Ways of Teaching: The Artistry of Teaching with Multiple Intelligences.* Palatine, Ill.: Skylight, 1991.

Model for a Student Journals

6. MULTIMODAL REFLECTION LOG*

 An insight or thought
I had today is . . .
(Write it)

An interesting pattern
I observe is . . .
(Think about it)

An image I have
of today is . . .
(Draw it)

A gesture or movement
for today is . . .
(Do it)

If today were a song
it would be . . .
(Sing it)

My feelings about
today are . . .
(Meditate on them)

I want to talk with
someone about . . .
(Discuss it)

* This model is adapted from Lazear, David. *Seven Ways of Knowing: Teching for Multiple Intelligences.*
Palatine, Ill.: Skylight, 1991

Transfer of Learning

Many cognitive researchers suggest that students have really learned something *only* when they can transfer that learning to situations beyond the formal school setting. In other words, if we can catch students making applications we can assess their grasp of concepts we have been teaching. Helping students transfer involves several tasks: (1) helping them make connections among things they have learned within a given subject area, (2) helping them make connections between one subject area and another, and (3) helping them connect their learning with life beyond the classroom.

Robin Fogarty (1987) describes the issue of transfer:

> In some cases the transfer of learning is obvious because the learned skills seem close to the skill situation in which they are used or transferred. For example, when teaching "supermarket math"—price comparisons, making change, etc.—the learning situation "hugs" the life situation. The transfer is clear. This transfer is called simple transfer.
>
> However, in other instances, the learning in the school situation seems far removed or remote from the transfer across content into life. For example, a high school student spends a great deal of time and energy staring at, memorizing and using the Periodic Table of Elements. . . .
>
> Most students do not "see" how this learning is useful. The transfer is complex. . . . The transfer here is remote; it is obscure. The student needs explicit instruction in making these and other connections. In these situations, teachers can help kids make relevant transfer through mediation or "bridging" strategies. (278)

Following is a model, based on the research of Robin Fogarty, that analyzes student learning from the perspective of transfer and suggests strategies for increasing student transfer. The formula I am suggesting here is *the greater the transfer the greater the learning*. Once we have assessed a student's level of transfer, we can deepen and expand the student's learning by increasing the level of transfer. Keep in mind that it is important to honor the individuality of students in their capacity to transfer their learning. Our goal should be to help them increase transfer one stage at a time. (Unfortunately, given the current national preoccupation with test scores and our bias toward standardized tests, teaching for transfer must also help students bridge their learning so that they are successful on a wide range of such tests.)

Multiple Intelligence Approaches to Assessment © 1994 Zephyr Press, Tucson, Arizona

STAGES OF LEARNING TRANSFER

Stage Description	Recognition Clues	Key "Increasing Transfer" Strategy
SLEEPER Misses the point of what is being studied. Sees no connections or possible uses for the information in a lesson.	"These are interesting ideas, but what good are they?" "Why do we have to learn this stuff anyway?" "This lesson is boring. I'll never need this."	Make connections for them by telling them ways the information can help them. Help them see ways they can use information from a lesson beyond school. Have them discuss with their peers in the class the importance of what was learned in a lesson.
DUPLICATOR Is excited by what was learned in a lesson and wants to tell others about it in exactly the same way as it was originally presented.	"I can't wait to tell my parents and friends about this!" "Could I have a copy of your overhead or a clean copy of the work sheet?" "Say that again so I can write it down," or "Tell me the steps for doing this again," or "Please let me copy your notes."	Question their understanding of the overhead or work sheet and have them explain it in their own words. Role-play sharing what you have learned with people who weren't in the classroom with you today.
REPLICATOR Understands applications of what was learned as long as the subject context and situation are the same as in the original learning situation.	"That's a great idea! I plan to use it as often as I can." "I understand as long as I'm in school, but I lose it outside." "I understand in this subject area, but I don't in others."	Help them discover appropriate applications beyond the content area of the initial learning. Work to help them make creative or "tangential" applications of something learned in a lesson.
STRATEGIST Takes information from a lesson or something learned in the classroom and uses it in a variety of different settings and situations.	"I can see many ways to use what I have learned in this lesson." "What I've learned in this lesson is the same thing I learned in another subject." "What I've learned is going to help with a challenge I'm facing outside of school."	Work to expand their lists of new application ideas. Celebrate interdisciplinary connections they have seen and help them discover others. Help them learn to evaluate appropriate applications of different things learned (when, where, and how to use them most effectively).
CREATOR Uses information from a lesson as a springboard to creative and original thinking; sees unusual connections and patterns in the information.	"What we just learned got me thinking about something that was not part of the lesson." "What if you took this idea we just learned and linked it with other ideas from other lessons?" "I've been thinking about what we studied yesterday and have some new thoughts about it."	Encourage them to find unusual connections between their learning and other things and to look for subtle patterns in their thinking. Ask them to experiment with communicating their learning to other people (for example, someone much younger or much older, someone from a different culture and socioeconomic group, or someone with little formal education).

Anecdotal Reporting Model

Everyone loves a good story. Anecdotal reporting is a matter of creating a story of students' academic progress, cognitive maturation, capacity/competency expansion, and overall human development. This form of reporting is already a small, although usually secondary, part of most of our current report card models. I am suggesting that this dimension needs to be expanded and should be a record of a teacher's observations of a student's academic and cognitive capacity and general human development during an entire grading period. In fact, on the report cards we send home, this dimension of reporting should have equal or greater weight than letter or numerical grades.

The model on page 167 is based on an anecdotal reporting approach developed by a teacher at the Governor Bent Elementary School in Albuquerque, New Mexico. This teacher carries a small spiral notebook in his hip pocket during the day. The notebook contains a section for each student and has anecdotal categories such as "Asked me," "Wanted to try," "Wondered about," and so on. During the course of a week, the teacher records something about each student as he observes them in the act of learning, processing information, playing on the playground, and interacting with other students. This is not as big a job as it may seem at first glance, especially if it is done on a daily or weekly basis at the time you make the observation. When it comes time to send home a report card, you can simply photocopy the appropriate pages from your notebook for each student and include them with the letter/numerical reports.

The following chart is intended to provide some beginning ideas for initiating an anecdotal reporting process for your students. The key is to get started! Don't try to report everything at first. Choose what will be relatively easy given your current teaching practices, and allow the process to expand naturally as you become more familiar with the process and as your own awareness of the need for telling the whole learning story increases.

Anecdotal Reporting Model

Cognitive Patterns	"Transfer" Ability	MI Capacity Development	Social Interactions	Other Observations
Had many questions about . . . Evaluated own performance on . . . Asked for help in understanding how to think about . . .	Told parents or siblings about . . . Saw connections beyond school for . . . Tried to apply something from one subject to another by . . .	Improved intelligence skill(s) of . . . Wanted to know how to get better at . . . Approached a task in a new way by . . .	Talked with friends about . . . Exhibited new social skills when . . . Played a new or different role in a group by . . .	Wanted more information about . . . Asked if he or she could try . . . Found it humorous (or upsetting) that . . .

Domain Projects, Exhibits, Performances, and Displays

Projects, exhibits, performances, and displays are at the center of disciplines such as the performing arts, the visual arts, and sports. Howard Gardner (1991) talks about these "domain projects":

> *Domain projects* are extended curricular sequences based upon a concept or practice that is central to a discipline; examples include composition in the visual arts, rehearsal in music, writing an opening scene in imaginative writing. In a domain project, which can run from a few days to a few weeks, students encounter this central practice in a number of different ways and have ample opportunities to assume the stances of producing, perceiving, and reflection. Students also encounter many opportunities for assessment—self assessment and assessment by peers, as well as assessment by teachers and even by outside experts. . . .
>
> Domain projects are evaluated on a number of domain-appropriate dimensions, with developmental scales employed as a means of assessing the students' emerging competence. (239)

Other examples could include the public exhibition of one's art or photography, the performance of a dance routine or drama for an audience, the competitive sports game, and so on. In chapter 5, I suggested that such things as projects, performances, exhibits, and displays provide us with an important model for designing new forms of assessment in the so-called academic disciplines. Domain projects are to a certain degree simulations of the discipline in real life beyond the formal education setting. Students are provided an opportunity to crawl inside the various practices of a discipline for a long enough period of time that they gain some skill in working with the media of the discipline, the various thought processes involved, the evaluative standards of the discipline, and so on. But what is probably even more significant from the standpoint of student learning and motivation, students are given time and assistance in producing something that is meaningful and significant to them.

Following are some suggestions for implementing domain projects, performances, displays, and exhibits in the different academic areas.

Domain Project, Performance, Display, and Exhibit Ideas*

LANGUAGE ARTS	HISTORY	MATHEMATICS
Hold **public readings** in which students present their writing (essays, stories, poetry, and plays)	Conduct **historical research projects** in which students investigate people, events, places, and things that they find interesting	Design **math in everyday life exhibits** to show practical applications of math in daily living.
Schedule **formal speaking engagements** for students to speak to organizations, clubs, or groups in school and in the community.	Create **living historical museum displays** that simulate an era; invite the public, other classes, other grade levels, and other schools to visit.	Design a **math olympics competition** with events such as calculation skills, problem solving, algebraic processes, and math proofs.
Stage **formal debates** on topics of concern to students; students must do the research and defend their ideas and opinions.	Research, write, and perform **historical docudramas** for lower grades and community organizations.	Create **math-process board games** that require the players to use and execute various math processes.
Publish **students' writing** in school or parent newsletters, in the local newspaper, or in a library comprised of their own work.	Conduct **analyses of current historical trends** based on "learnings from the past" (for example, does history repeat itself?).	Write and publish a **students-created math textbook** that explains math concepts, processes, and operations in ways other students can understand.

* For the most part, the living skills (including shop, home economics, computer science, physical education, and driver's education) and the fine arts (including dance, drama, instrumental and vocal music, art, photography) are by nature well grounded in domain project, performance, exhibit, and display approaches to assessing students' progress in these subject areas. In many ways, they provide many helpful authentic, intelligence-based models that I believe we should emulate in the so-called academic areas.

     Multiple Intelligence Approaches to Assessment © 1994 Zephyr Press, Tucson, Arizona

Domain Project, Performance, Display, and Exhibit Ideas *(continued)*

SCIENCE/HEALTH	GLOBAL STUDIES
Design **hands-on health fairs** to promote more healthful living in the school, family, and community.	Plan **cultural immersion festivals** in which students must embody various cultural values, mores, perspectives, and understandings.
Invent a **new product** based on performing a scientific experiment or one that incorporates key scientific concepts and processes.	Design **world problems exhibits** to show personal knowledge, interest, opinions, and possible solutions for key issues facing the planet today.
Publish student-created **healthy living brochures, articles, and posters;** distribute them to the school and community at large.	Write and publish **cultural sensitivity handbooks** to help others honor the unique gifts, perspectives, beliefs, and values of various cultures.
Create a **science museum or exploratorium** in which participants can experience different scientific concepts and discoveries in a hands-on manner.	Design **world geography games and puzzles** that require participants to use and develop their knowledge of the world in the playing of the games.

Epilogue

Redefining the Boundaries of Education

The Need for "Assessment Literacy" Training

An issue that often gets in the way of moving assessment in genuinely new directions in our schools is the issue of "assessment literacy." According to Richard J. Stiggins, director of the Center for Performance Assessment, Northwest Regional Educational Laboratory in Portland, Oregon, assessment literacy involves training in being a critical consumer of various assessment data we receive. This is a crucial issue for educators, students, parents, members of school boards, legislators, and other public officials. In "Assessment Literacy," an article that appeared in the March 1991 *Kappan* magazine, Stiggins asks us to analyze our assessment literacy as a society through a series of penetrating questions*:

* The questions are Richard Stiggins' and the commentary is the author's.

- **Who trains students to be critical consumers of the feedback provided by their teachers? Who prepares students to act in their own best interests when it comes to the evaluation of their achievement?**

The answer is no one. What this means is that students can find themselves victims of unfair reports of their achievement and have little or no recourse to alternative, more authentic means for demonstrating their achievement. Unfortunately students often buy the subtle message that is communicated through a low grade—that they are stupid or incapable.

Due to a lack of training in authentic assessment, many teachers are also threatened by the suggestions that students should have a say in how they will be assessed and that feedback from students on *how* they learn may be as valid and important as the teacher's feedback on *what* they supposedly have (or have not) learned.

- **Who teaches parents to understand the meaning of grades or test scores that are sent home? Who trains parents to ask the probing questions of a critical consumer of data?**

Of course, the answer, once again, is no one. Unfortunately, what this means is that parents are forced to take test scores at face value and to accept others' interpretations of what the scores mean. Also, parents rarely get reports on areas in which their children are succeeding if these areas don't fall within the traditional categories of the verbally and mathematically biased report card. Given the current deficit-based approach to assessment in American education, this means that parents often become preoccupied with areas of their children's weaknesses and miss the areas of success and achievement.

- **Who helps members of school boards or others in the community to understand the meaning of high-quality assessments, and who helps them to arm their assessment alarm system?**

Again, the answer is no one! Society's assessment illiteracy is evident when test scores are published in local newspapers and are used as a basis for the competitive evaluation of various schools within a district. In some states, school boards and administrators have even gone so far as to use test scores as the basis for hiring and firing principals and for determining teachers' salaries.

- **Who takes responsibility for the assessment literacy of legislators or other public officials?**

Multiple Intelligence Approaches to Assessment © 1994 Zephyr Press, Tucson, Arizona

No one! Unfortunately, these people, who often control policy making and funding for education, have little or no understanding of current educational research, and therefore they make decisions in a vacuum. Far too often, decisions are legislated that are not in the best interests of students and the education process.

As I mentioned earlier, we are at a point in educational research where we know much more than we have ever known before about good teaching and the learning process. Why is this information not part of the discussions of public officials as they are making decisions that are related to education? Why are teachers not consulted when decisions are being made that affect the lives of our children? Teachers must be brought to the center of the education reform process. They are professionals who know what it takes to reach and teach children in the formal educational process.

A final observation from Richard Stiggins (1991) summarizes this discussion:

> All who presume to assess, evaluate, and act on student achievement data must come to understand the full range of possible student achievement targets and assessment methods at our disposal. . . . There are as many domains of knowledge to be mastered as there are school subjects. Students need to be able to think and solve problems in each of those content domains. Our expectations regarding desirable behaviors include psychomotor skills, communication skills, artistic skills, and more. And the products we expect students to create range from written papers and reports to science projects and works of art. . . .
>
> The assessment-literate person can describe the achievement targets in any specific context in specific terms. He or she can describe the knowledge to be learned, the forms of thinking to be mastered, the particular behaviors to be demonstrated, and the products to be created. A person who is assessment literate realizes that effective instruction, learning, and assessment are all impossible without these specifications. (535)

Catalyzing the Change

In light of the findings of contemporary educational research, people often ask why schools have not changed more dramatically than they have. Why are the appropriate and well-documented new educational practices not being implemented?

Part of the problem may be our own misconceptions about the process of change itself. Change in any organization is usually slow, painful, and difficult, even in the face of the best research that clearly indicates the new directions needed. We often become impatient and want to implement major changes all at once, thus missing significant change that may be occurring on a smaller scale right before our eyes. Sometimes the difficulty is that people simply are not aware of the latest research findings that show there are effective ways to reach all students. In this case, often a simple sharing with professional colleagues, parents, and the general public, in practical ways they can understand, makes a world of difference.

In my own professional journey I have tried to be an agent of change in many organizations, including churches, nonindustrialized villages, major corporations and businesses, school districts and individual schools, and public and private service agencies. I have observed an interesting and very encouraging pattern of people's relationship to change—a pattern I have come to trust over the years:

About 10 percent of any organization's members are already awake. They are the movers and shakers. They are forever seeking better ways of doing things. They are the experimenters, risk takers, and innovators, and they are willing to try almost anything new that holds promise for enhancing creativity, human growth, and productivity. They will spend hours and days attending workshops and seminars, often at their own expense, in order to expand their awareness and to push the edges of their own professional development.

About 10 percent of any organization's members are asleep and are deeply committed to remaining in this state. They often respond to the findings of contemporary educational research by saying such things as, "There is really nothing new under the sun. Everything that is 'hot' in education today is simply a matter of new labels on old things we have been doing for years. Anyway, I'm already doing all of this supposedly 'new stuff' and have been for years." They dismiss the findings of contemporary research by erroneously assuming that today's facts are simply a repackaging of the old, traditional ways. Unfortunately, this response is often a masked defense that really means, "I don't have to (and don't what to) change."

About 80 percent of any organization's members are asleep but "awakeable." For the most part they are not interested in attending professional development workshops and seminars. They often respond to suggestions of change with, "The old ways have worked for years. Why change something that has always worked? Don't fix it if it ain't broke!" What they often fail to grasp is that the world context in which education takes place today is brand new, and the old ways are "broke"! Today's students live in a world different from the one we lived in. They face challenges today that did not exist when the so-called traditional wisdom was popular and when it did work. However, this 80 percent is not vocationally committed to the "old ways" position. These people are potentially open to considering and trying new ways if such ways can be shown to work and to be at least as effective as the old ways.

I believe that it is on this 80 percent that we should focus our energy. Often the key issue in working with this segment of our schools is the issue of transfer or the practical implications and applications of the research. We must learn to honor and respect individuals at whatever point they stand in the change process, and we must work with them in ways that are appropriate for them and that will help them take one more step in a new direction. While change is difficult and often painful, it can also be fun, exciting, challenging, creative, and personally rewarding.

Fourteen Things You Can Do Right Now
(without asking anyone's permission and without endangering your job!)

1. **Teach students ABOUT multiple intelligences.** Design a series of mini-lessons or activities whose purpose is to help students get to know themselves intellectually. Regularly expose them to the concept of "seven ways of knowing," and help them get increasingly better at using all seven ways (see *Seven Pathways of Learning: Teaching Students and Parents about Multiple Intelligences* [Lazear 1994] for ideas.)

2. **Vary your instruction by teaching WITH multiple intelligences.** Within the course of a week, make sure you teach lessons that give students opportunities to use all seven intelligences to gain the knowledge and understanding you are trying to impart and to process the information in a lesson. (See *Seven Ways of Teaching: Teaching with Multiple Intelligences* [Lazear 1991] for multiple intelligence lesson ideas for various subject areas.)

3. **Provide homework assignments that require students to work in the various intelligence areas.** Create fun, unusual, and interesting homework assignments that will stretch students to use all seven intelligences. Steer away from drill assignments and move into the realms of higher-order thinking and creativity. Be sure that you inform parents in advance that you will be assigning such work, and tell them why and how it will benefit their children.

4. **Give unit tests or daily quizzes that are multiperceptual.** Use the "MI Assessment Instruments Menu" (chapter 6) to design exciting, challenging, and enjoyable activities through which students can "prove" their knowledge. Be sure that you have spent time teaching them about the seven intelligences and that they have had a chance to use all seven ways of knowing in your classroom before you spring these kinds of tests or quizzes on them.

5. **Have conferences or in-services with parents about multiple intelligences.** Create a special awareness workshop for parents that will help them understand the theory of multiple intelligences and how you are using it in your teaching and classroom. (*Seven Pathways of Learning* [Lazear 1994] contains a series of "Notes to Parents" that can help.) At parent-teacher conferences, report on the full intellectual development of their child. You might show parents the intelligence profile indicator for their child and ask for feedback on things they know about their child that can help you reach and teach him or her more effectively.

6. **Start students building and keeping portfolios, process-folios, and journals and logs.** Refer to the models in chapter 7 and adapt them to something with which you are comfortable and that you believe will work with your students. Remember that what you are after is helping students create a holistic picture of their learning journey. Let them decide what to include as long as it gives an accurate picture of what they have done, what they have learned, and how they have progressed. (At parent-teacher conferences, consider having students talk to their parents about their portfolios, process-folios, and journals.)

7. **Begin building a set of student intelligence profiles.** Using student observation techniques such as those suggested in chapter 3 (or create your own), practice carefully observing your students as they are involved in a variety of activities and learning tasks, including when they are relating to each other and when they are at play. Watch for manifestations of the seven intelligences. Keep a record of your observations, using something such as the "MI Profile Indicator" on page 71, then use these observations to help you more effectively teach and reach your students.

8. **Integrate teaching the core capacities of the seven intelligences into your curriculum.** Every day give students opportunities to awaken their intelligences and to practice using them in daily lessons. This will help them strengthen, enhance, and expand their full intellectual potential. (See *Seven Ways of Knowing: Teaching for Multiple Intelligences* [Lazear 1991] for awakening exercises, amplifying practices, model lessons, and transfer strategies.)

9. **Set up "intelligence stations" or make sure the "media" of all the intelligences are available to students.** If you are an elementary teacher you could set up stations that contain the media of the different ways of knowing. Allow students to do their daily classroom work in these stations, using the tools of each station. If you are a secondary level teacher and you do not have your own classroom, you may need to have a set of intelligence kitbags that you carry with you from class to class. These should contain the materials, supplies, and tools of the various intelligences.

10. **Initiate the practice of "anecdotal reporting" on your students.** In some way that is comfortable and easy for you, regularly record what you are observing and learning about your students as you work with them in your class. (See the "Anecdotal Reporting" model in chapter 7 for an example of how to do this). You do not have to make an anecdotal entry for every student every day, but you should probably make at least one per student each week.

11. **Send home "intelligence development reports" along with the regular report card.** In addition to the required periodic report cards that are sent home for parents, include an additional report that tells about students' intelligence capacity development (see chapter 2 and the Appendix for some models that you can adapt to help you get started on this). Steer away from "deficit-based" reporting (that is, using language that suggests learning disabilities, problems, or weaknesses). Focus instead on the developmental aspects of students' learning (that is, using language that reveals students' interest levels, their strengths, and their comfort zones).

12. **Invite students' input on designing examinations.** Prior to a formal examination period, ask students to tell you what would help them show you what they know. Then using this information, create a test, with options, that takes into account their input. Your goal should be to maximize the possibility of all students succeeding on the test; therefore, the test should contain multiple ways for them to prove their knowledge and understanding. Remember that not all students must (or will) prove themselves in the same way.

13. **Experiment with "domain" projects, displays, exhibits, and performances.** As a culminating activity for a unit, have students create a major presentation that integrates the knowledge base of the unit and that uses all seven intelligences (for example, specify that their project, display, exhibit, or performance must include each of the intelligences). The criteria for the presentations should go beyond mere factual recall to include implications, applications, and the transfer of learning; in other words, they must demonstrate genuine understanding of the material.

14. **Share with a trusted colleague something new you have tried.** Candidly discuss both the pluses and minuses with this person and reflect with him or her on what you have learned about the art of teaching from your experiment. Invite feedback. Don't ask the other person to buy the whole ball of wax of multiple intelligences; rather, take it a step at a time and ask that person to share what he or she might be willing to try based on what you have shared.

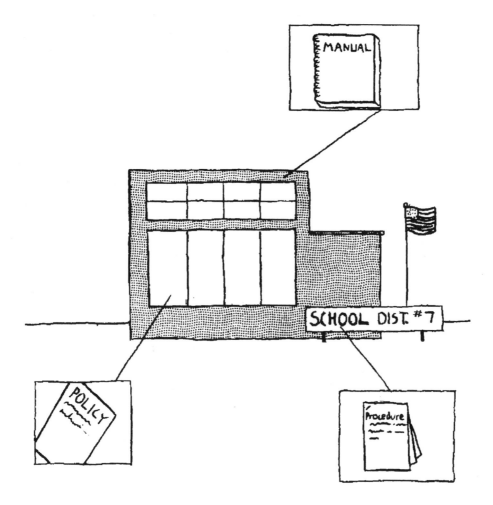

District Policy Restructuring
(Brain-Based, Research-Based Assessment Procedures)

The time is now for re-creating both our assessment philosophy and the assessment process in American education. I am mostly concerned with those who are involved with assessment at the practitioner level, namely, teachers, principals, school counselors, district-level curriculum and staff development administrators, and superintendents. Following are beginning practices that I believe can help move us from a society preoccupied with formal testing to one that is concerned with learning and the authentic assessment of what students know. These kinds of practices should be at the center of school board discussions about policy making, school reform and restructuring. They should also be guidelines for assessment literacy training for both educators and the general public.

■ **Assessment practices in our schools should mirror assessment in the so-called real world beyond school.** The vast majority of formal testing we do in our schools is quite artificial when placed alongside the realities of the contemporary workplace. In school, when it is time for a test, students are told to put away their resource materials and work by themselves without talking to or getting ideas from others. The testing situation is special and isolated from the learning situation, and the teacher and other students may not coach each other (this is called cheating). Perhaps the only time we are tested in this way outside of school is when we get our driver's license! Most of the times we are assessed are on the job and in situations that are specifically related to improving projects or our performance. In these situations we are encouraged to have our best resources very much at hand, and we are encouraged to rely on others and use others on our team.

Project Spectrum, an early childhood assessment project based on multiple intelligences, suggests that assessment in school should mirror the way it happens beyond the school setting. This would mean blurring the lines between the curriculum and assessment. There would not be special testing situations, for assessment would always be occurring as students are involved in various problem-solving tasks or learning activities, while they are at play, or when they are immersed in a particular lesson. Assessment would become as much a part of teaching as direct instruction, and the primary task of assessment would be in the hands of teachers who are intimately involved in the lives of their students rather than in the hands of external testing organizations.

■ **Assessment should be individualized and conducted in ways and with instruments that are developmentally appropriate.** Assessment should not be something we do TO students. Students must become active partners with us in demonstrating what they are learning. Assessment should be something we do WITH students. There are at least two implications of this participatory approach to assessment: (1) we must take the individual differences among students very seriously, and (2) we must expand our awareness of developmental psychology to include the development of at least the seven intelligences. As I mentioned earlier, there are no standard students, so why should we think we must have standard tests?

Lest I be misunderstood, I am NOT suggesting there should be no standards that students should be expected to meet. Quite the contrary. My point is that standardized tests do not tell us if students have met the standards! In virtually every workshop I conduct in schools and districts across North America, teachers are terribly frustrated by the addiction we seem to have to test scores in America. Rarely do we question what these scores actually tell us about what students have learned or what they are equipped to do beyond our schools. And rarely do we ask what damage they may be doing to students, in terms both of their self-esteem and their motivation for learning.

However, I believe that it may not be as difficult as we think to turn the tables and move our current assessment practices in some dramatically new directions. What if students were involved in designing tests through which they knew they could prove to us that they have met the standards? What if parents were part of the assessment process? What if students were permitted to master different "standards" when they were psychologically and motivationally ready to do so? And what if the "standard" of standardized testing required students to demonstrate their understanding of a subject in a variety of ways?

- **Make authentic, intelligence-based assessment central to the educational process.** Assessment (if it is authentic *and* intelligence based) should drive the curriculum. It should be central to instruction. In fact, we should teach to the test (*if* it is authentic *and* intelligence based). A good model for this is how we teach the performing arts or how we coach people involved in sports. In these areas our concern is to prepare someone for a musical recital, a theatrical production, a competitive sports event, an art exhibit, and so on.

Any test we give should be worth taking; the motivation should be intrinsic to the test itself. In other words, doing well on the test is its own reward. Tests should be graduated by degrees of difficulty, and students should be allowed to choose which level of a test to take, as well as when they feel ready to take it. Not all students are ready to be tested on the same material at the same time, in the same way. Furthermore, students should not be penalized for trying a test that is more difficult than they may be able to handle. This test should be seen as a chance for students to understand what will eventually be required of them.

- **Assessment practices should be designed for the benefit of students.** This means that, by design, tests should be learning experiences. They should challenge students to demonstrate fully their knowledge and skill in a particular area. Taking the test should be an enhancement and celebration of what students have learned. Tests should give students a chance to show off. A test should be something students look forward to. It should be an occasion for them to take pride in demonstrating what they have achieved and what they have learned.

Students should be able to take the same test as many times as is necessary to complete it satisfactorily (as in an apprenticeship program). We should do away with secret questions on tests and with hidden criteria or standards. Everyone should know what is on each test at each level of difficulty and what the standards are for successful completion of a given test. If tests are authentic, this is not a problem. Consider again the performing arts or sports. In these areas people are crystal clear about exactly what is involved in the "test" (that is, their performance). We need to design the equivalent of this type of test for all so-called academic areas.

- **Teachers should be central to the assessment process, both in the design and the execution.** Testing organizations are obviously external to the teaching and learning situation. Authentic testing is a very subjective matter in that, if we are genuinely concerned with finding out what students really know and understand, someone who has intimate knowledge about the students to be tested must be involved to ensure that students are thoroughly and fairly examined. As I have said many times, a "correct answer" demonstrates neither knowledge nor understanding, and an "incorrect answer" does not necessarily mean lack of knowledge or understanding. Teachers are highly skilled professionals who have been involved at every juncture with their students in the educational journey. They can be trusted to know their students (better than any outside "objective" agent) and to know how to ensure that their students are thoroughly and fairly examined.

Teachers must be given time to create and administer authentic tests. They must be given time to work with each other to create tests that are challenging, motivating, and worth taking. The testing situation should involve a panel of judges, as in the Olympics, to ensure an objective and fair performance evaluation that maintains the high standards and criteria of the discipline being tested. Examination panels could be made up of people who know the students (their daily classroom teachers), experts in the field from the community (who know the required performance standards of the discipline beyond the formal school setting), and other teachers in the department and from other departments (who know the diploma and performance standards of the school and district).

■ **Institute multiperceptual testing practices throughout the district or system**. The concept of multiperceptual testing, presented in chapter 6, may be the single most important and revolutionary idea presented in this book. It presupposes an equality among the different intelligences or ways of knowing, thus overcoming the verbal-linguistic and logical-mathematical bias of 99.9 percent of current testing practices. Students can know, understand, perceive, and express their learning deeply and fully through each of the intelligences!

Multiperceptual assessment assumes that one's learning is valid regardless of how something was learned and whether or not it can be reproduced on standardized tests. It assumes that assessment instruments and processes must be intelligence fair if they are to be accurate measures of students' knowledge and understanding. In chapter 6 I presented suggestions for a series of new testing instruments for each intelligence, as well as specific applications of the instruments for different academic subject areas. Here I simply wish to underscore the importance of testing instruments and processes that genuinely embody the unique language, symbol system, media, and cognitive processes of the different intelligences.

Implicit in the idea of multiperceptual assessment is the suggestion that we need to provide students with a variety of options by which they can successfully demonstrate their mastery of certain concepts, processes, ideas, facts, and operations. It likewise suggests that if we can indeed couch assessment in the language and symbol systems of the different intelligences, we will dramatically improve the success rate of students in our schools and show a very different picture from the standard, predictable bell-shaped curve (which does not allow for the success of all students or give us accurate information about what students can do with the information they have supposedly learned).

One of my favorite passages, on which my philosophy of education is based and which sums up the emerging new paradigm of human development (and which I have shared in each of my previous books) was written by William James. He says: "I have no doubt whatever that most people live . . . in a very restricted circle of their potential being. They make use of a very small portion of their possible consciousness . . . much like a person who, out of the whole body organism, should get into the habit of using and moving only the little finger. We all have reservoirs of life to draw upon of which we do not dream" (Harman 1988). I believe that, of all professionals in our society, it is educators whose main responsibility is to help people tap their fullest potential as human beings.

Appendix

Kindergarten Progress Report*

Student Name _____

Telephone _____ Birth Date _____

Recognizes (R) and Prints (P) Numerals

	R	P			R	P			R	P			R	P
1				6				11				16		
2				7				12				17		
3				8				13				18		
4				9				14				19		
5				10				15				20		

Alphabet

■	Letter	■	Letter	Sound
A		a		
B		b		
C		c		
D		d		
E		e		
F		f		
G		g		
H		h		
I		i		
J		j		
K		k		
L		l		
M		m		
N		n		
O		o		
P		p		
Q		q		
R		r		
S		s		
T		t		
U		u		
V		v		
W		w		
X		x		
Y		y		
Z		z		

COUNTS ORALLY

Fall	1	to	_____
Winter	1	to	_____
Spring	1	to	_____

KEY FOR MULTIPLE ABILITIES

	Not Being Evaluated
L	Low interest
C	Consistent growth
S	High interest/Strength

* Used by permission of Harley Harmon Elementary School, Clark County School District

Kindergarten Progress Report *(continued)*

Linguistic Intelligence

Reading

	1	2	3
Has desire to read; looks at books			
Puts events in sequence			
Identifies sight words			
Identifies letter sounds in words			
Recognizes cover, front, back, and title of book			
Proceeds from left to right			

Writing

	1	2	3
Copies print from the environment			
Spaces words			
Uses known words			
Expresses thoughts in writing or pictures			
Prints first name			
Prints last name			

Speaking

	1	2	3
Shares experiences in a group			
Uses complete sentences			

Listening

	1	2	3
Listens to stories			
Follows simple directions			
Identifies rhyming words			

Interpersonal Intelligence

	1	2	3
Follows rules			
Displays appropriate attention span			
Walks and plays cooperatively			
Uses self-control			
Knows address			
Knows phone number			

Bodily-Kinesthetic Intelligence

	1	2	3
Displays large motor skills (hop, skip, jump, balance)			
Displays fine motor skills (cut, draw, write, color)			

Musical-Rhythmic Intelligence

	1	2	3
Appreciates music			
Can hold pitch, stick to rhythm			

Spatial Intelligence

	1	2	3
Assembles objects			
Produces art			

Mathematical Intelligence

	1	2	3
Recognizes shapes			
Recognizes colors			
Sorts and classifies			
Understands concept of more			
Understands concept of less			
Understands a pattern			

Matches numbers to objects

1   2   3   4   5   6   7   8   9   10

Kindergarten Progress Report (continued)

Teacher _____

Principal _____ **Year** _____

Comments

Fall

Winter

Spring

Assigned to _____

Attendance:	Present	Absent	Total
1st semester			
2nd semester			
TOTAL			

Kindergarten Spectrum Report*

Name: _____ **Date:** _____

Teacher: _____

Attendance: Days absent _____ **Days tardy** _____

S = Strength, high interest   A = Appropriate for grade/age   L = Low interest

Logical-Mathematical

Ability to use a notation system, organize number information, develop patterns, estimate, solve math-oriented problems

Engagement in math activities	S A L
Use of math manipulatives	S A L
Organization of math information	S A L

Comments:

Linguistic

Use of vocabulary, sentence structure, sense of story, expressiveness, sequencing structure

Engagement in language activities	S A L
Expressive language skills	S A L
Receptive language skills	S A L

Comments:

Bodily-Kinesthetic

Control of movement, balance, rhythm sensitivity, use of space, unique movement ideas

Engagement in movement activities	S A L
Gross motor control	S A L
Unique use of space and body	S A L

Comments:

Musical

Music perception and production, pitch recognition, song reproduction, tempo, rhythm, pitch in singing

Engagement in music activities	S A L
Use of musical instruments	S A L
Use of voice	S A L

Comments:

* Used by permission of Gloucester Spectrum Project

Spatial

A. Art: Use of color, design, line, composition, detail in drawing
B. Assembly: Construction, cause and effect, mechanical ability, fine motor control, systematic approach

Engagement in art activities	S A L
Engagement in assembly activities	S A L
Use of color, line, design	S A L
Systematic approach to cause and effect problems	S A L
Fine motor control	S A L

Comments:

Social

A. Intrapersonal: understands self, knows likes and dislikes, knows strengths, likes to work and play alone
B. Interpersonal: understands others, sees social problems and solutions, likes to work and play with other children

Engagement in social activities	S A L
Understanding of self	S A L
Understanding of others	S A L
Social problem solving	S A L

Comments:

Related Skills

Color, number, and letter recognition	Independence
Visual-Perceptual motor skills	Self-control
Memory for auditory and visual information	Ability to focus and attend

Kindergarten Spectrum Report *(continued)*

Linguistic Intelligence Score Sheet

Student's name: _____ **Date:** _____

Vocabulary 1 simple 2 more descriptive 3 variety, adjectives, mood setting	**Sentence Structure** 1 simple 2 includes prepositional phrases, compound sentences 3 uses clauses (because, that, if, -ing)
Temporal Markers 1 simple, sequential 2 some logical connections, time, adverbs 3 consistent	**Narrative Voice** 1 seldom 2 some elaboration 3 frequent: descriptive; uses metaphors, similes
Dialogue 1 little or none 2 brief conversation 3 sustains dialogue	**Thematic Coherence** 1 undeveloped transitions 2 mini-stories 3 coherent, consistent, resolves story
Expressiveness 1 little or none 2 some vocal effects 3 consistent	**Primary Language Function** _____ storytelling _____ describing _____ reporting _____ investigating _____ labeling/categorizing _____ interacting with adult

Comments

Use of props:

Transformation of materials:

Skills from other domains:

Pupil Progress Report*

School _____ **Telephone Number** _____

School Year _____ **Students' Name** _____

Room _____ **Group** _____ **Date of Birth** _____

Teacher _____ **Principal** _____

To the parents or guardians:

The purpose of any reporting is to give you an accurate picture of your child's progress. It is hoped that the progress report being used this year, along with the parent/student/teacher conference system, will give you the kind of information that you, as parents, want to know about your child. Your child's progress will be measured on individual academic growth. We encourage you to call or visit the school any time you have a question about your child's school work. In addition, we also welcome your comments and suggestions on how to make this progress report more meaningful to you.

Superintendent

* Used by permission of Key School Option Program, Indianapolis Public Schools.

Pupil Progress Report (continued)

REPORTING PERIOD

_____ to _____

ATTENDANCE REPORT

	1	2	3	4	Final
Days absent (excused)					
Days absent (unexcused)					
Times tardy					

Upon evaluation of your child's physical, intellectual, and social development, as evidenced by this progress report, your child has been assigned to _____ for the next school year.

Evaluations are based on developmental performance descriptors

EVALUATION KEY

N Slow progress; needs help
S Steady progress
R Rapid progress
Participation (_See_ Definition of Terms)

DEFINITION OF TERMS

Progress is determined by three factors: documented class work, the Key School Developmental Performance Descriptors, and the chronological age of the student.

Slow progress; needs help
The student is making slow or negligible progress and, therefore, additional assistance is recommended.

Steady progress
The student is constantly improving at a steady rate along the developmental continuum.

Rapid progress
The student is performing at an accelerated rate along the developmental continuum for a student of his or her chronological age.

Shows exceptional promise
The student shows signs of early giftedness in a particular area of intelligence as recognized by a minimum of two adults who are experts in that particular area.

Participation
Active participation
△ **Intrinsically motivated:** Student shows enjoyment and involvement in activity for its own sake regardless of external support or punishment.
☐ **Extrinsically motivated:** Student responds only to teacher-initiated activities and reward systems.
Passive
○ Little or no effort to participate
Disruptive
✕ Interferes with others' ability to participate

Multiple Intelligence Approaches to Assessment © 1994 Zephyr Press, Tucson, Arizona

Pupil Progress Report *(continued)*

SEVEN INTELLIGENCES

LINGUISTIC

English   Teacher _____

    Listening.. _____

    Speaking .... _____

    Writing .... _____

    Reading .... _____

    Participation .... _____

Comments: _____

_____

_____

Spanish   Teacher _____

    Listening.. _____

    Speaking .... _____

    Writing .... _____

    Reading .... _____

    Participation .... _____

Comments: _____

_____

_____

LOGICAL-MATHEMATICAL

Mathematics   Teacher _____

    Number sense .... _____

    Computation .... _____

    Problem solving .... _____

    Measurement.................................... _____

    Participation .... _____

Comments: _____

_____

_____

Research   Teacher _____

    Multimedia .... _____

    Participation .... _____

Comments: _____

_____

_____

Science   Teacher _____

    Problem solving .... _____

    Participation .... _____

Comments: _____

_____

_____

MUSICAL

Music   Teacher _____

    Symbol system
       and composition .... _____

    History, literature,
       and repertoire .... _____

    Tool manipulation
       (using the voice or instrument) _____

    Self-evaluation .... _____

    Participation .... _____

Comments: _____

_____

_____

SPATIAL

Science   Teacher _____

    Environment .... _____

    Life cycle .... _____

    Participation .... _____

Comments: _____

_____

_____

Visual arts   Teacher _____

    Three-dimensional art .... _____

    Drawing .... _____

    Painting .... _____

    Design.. _____

    Aesthetics .... _____

    Art history .... _____

    Self-evaluation .... _____

    Participation .... _____

Comments: _____

_____

_____

Geography   Teacher _____

    Locations .... _____

    Participation .... _____

Comments: _____

_____

_____

Pupil Progress Report *(continued)*

SEVEN INTELLIGENCES

BODILY-KINESTHETIC

Physical education   Teacher _____
    Bodily awareness
      and movement .... _____
    Physical fitness management........ _____
    Group interaction management ... _____
    Participation................................ _____
Comments: _____
_____
_____

Health   Teacher _____
    Nutrition .... _____
    Wellness .... _____
    Community concerns .... _____
    Participation................................ _____
Comments: _____
_____
_____

INTERPERSONAL

Family life   Teacher _____
    Relationships............................... _____
    Participation................................ _____
Comments: _____
_____
_____

Learning Communities   Teacher _____
    Caring, empathy,
      and understanding..................... _____
    Negotiations .... _____
    Teamwork .... _____
    Leadership................................... _____
    Sharing resources .... _____
    Participation................................ _____
Comments: _____
_____
_____

History   Teacher _____
    The democratic idea .... _____
    Participation................................ _____
Comments: _____
_____
_____

INTRAPERSONAL

Flow activity   Teacher _____
    Choices.. _____
    Participation................................ _____
Comments: _____
_____

Pods (_____) Teacher _____
    Strengths .... _____
    Participation................................ _____
Comments: _____
_____

Projects (_____) Teacher _____
    Connections .... _____
    Self-knowledge............................ _____
    Participation................................ _____
Comments: _____
_____
_____

**SHOWS EXCEPTIONAL
PROMISE—MERITS
ADDITIONAL OPPORTUNITIES**

Teacher _____
Comments: _____
_____
_____

Parent/Teacher conference

_____

Parent's signature

_____

Teacher's signature

Multiple Intelligence Approaches to Assessment © 1994 Zephyr Press, Tucson, Arizona

Bibliography

Alverno College Faculty. *Assessment at Alverno College,* rev. ed. Milwaukee, Wis.: Alverno College, 1985.

Archibald, D. A., and F. Newmann. *Beyond Standardized Testing: Assessing Authentic Academic Achievement in the Secondary School.* Reston, Va.: National Association of Secondary School Principals, 1988.

Armstrong, T. *7 Kinds of Smart: Identifying and Developing Your Many Intelligences.* New York: Penguin Books, 1993.

———. *In Their Own Way: Discovering and Encouraging Your Child's Own Personal Learning Style.* Los Angeles: J. P. Tarcher, 1987.

Bellanca, J., and R. Fogarty. *Patterns for Thinking, Patterns for Transfer.* Palatine, Ill.: The IRI Group, 1987, 1989.

Beyer, B. *Practical Strategies for the Teaching of Thinking.* Boston: Allyn and Bacon, 1987.

Bloom, B. *Taxonomy of Educational Objectives.* New York: David McKay, 1956.

Bloom, B., G. Madaus, and J. T. Hastings. *Evaluation to Improve Learning.* New York: McGraw-Hill, 1981.

Bogen, J. *Some Educational Aspects of Hemispheric Socialization.* Pomona, New York: Dromenon, 1979.

Boulding, K. *The Image.* Ann Arbor: University of Michigan Press, 1966.

Brandt, R. "On Performance Assessment: A Conversation with Grant Wiggins," *Educational Leadership* 49, no. 8 (May 1992): 35–37.

Bruner, J. *Toward a Theory of Instruction.* Cambridge, Mass.: Belknap Press, 1975.

Bruner, J., J. Goodnow, and G. Austin. *A Study of Thinking.* New York: Wiley, 1956.

Burke, K. *How to Assess Thoughtful Outcomes.* Palatine, Ill.: IRI/Skylight Publishing, 1993.

Buzan, T. *Use Both Sides of Your Brain.* New York: Dutton, 1991.

Caine, R., and G. Caine. "Understanding a Brain-Based Approach to Learning and Teaching," *Educational Leadership* 48, no. 2 (1990): 66–70.

———. *Making Connections: Teaching and the Human Brain.* Alexandria, Va.: Association for Supervision and Curriculum Development, 1991.

Campbell, L., B. Campbell, and D. Dickinson. *Teaching and Learning through Multiple Intelligences.* Seattle: New Horizons for Learning, 1992.

Chapman, C. *If the Shoe Fits . . . How to Use Multiple Intelligences in the Classroom.* Palatine, Ill.: IRI/Skylight Publishing, 1993.

Clark, E., Jr. "The Search for a New Educational Paradigm," *If Minds Matter: A Foreword to the Future,* vol. 1. Palatine, Ill.: IRI/Skylight Publishing, 1992, 25–40.

Costa, A. *The School as a Home for the Mind.* Palatine, Ill.: IRI/Skylight Publishing, 1991.

———. *Developing Minds,* rev. ed. Alexandria, Va.: Association for Supervision and Curriculum Development, 1991.

Costa, A., and B. Kalick. "Reassessing Assessment," *If Minds Matter: A Foreword to the Future,* vol. 2. Palatine, Ill.: IRI/Skylight Publishing, 1992, 275–80.

Department of Education and Science. *National Curriculum: Task Group on Assessment and Testing.* Great Britain, 1988.

Dickinson, D., ed. *Creating the Future: Perspectives on Educational Change.* Aston Clinton, Bucks, U.K.: Accelerated Learning Systems Ltd., 1991.

———. "Technology and the Multiple Intelligences," *Intelligence Connections* 1, nos. 2 and 3 (1992).

———. "Learning for Life," *If Minds Matter: A Foreword to the Future,* vol. 1 (Palatine, Ill.: IRI/Skylight Publishing, 1992), 51–61.

Diez, M. E., and C. J. Moon. "What Do We Want Students to Know? . . . and Other Important Questions," *Educational Leadership* 49, no. 8 (May 1992): 38–41.

Ferguson, M. *The Acquarian Conspiracy: Personal and Social Transformation in the 1980s.* Los Angeles: J. P. Tarcher, 1980.

Feurerstein, R. *Instrumental Enrichment: An Intervention Program for Cognitive Modifiability.* Baltimore, Md.: University Park Press, 1980.

Gardner, H. "Developing the Spectrum of Human Intelligences: Teaching in the Eighties, a Need to Change," *Harvard Educational Review* 57 (1987): 87–93.

———. *Developmental Psychology: An Introduction.* Boston: Little Brown, 1982.

———. *Frames of Mind: The Theory of Multiple Intelligences.* New York: Basic Books, 1983.

———. *Multiple Intelligences: The Theory in Practice.* New York: Basic Books, 1993.

———. *The Unschooled Mind: How Children Think and How Schools Should Teach.* New York: Basic Books, 1991.

Glasser, W. *Control Theory in the Classroom.* New York: Perennial Library, 1986.

Glickman, C. "Pretending Not to Know What We Know," *Educational Leadership* 48, no. 8 (May 1991): 4–9.

Gorman, B., and W. Johnson. *Successful Schooling for Everyone.* Bloomington, Ind.: National Education Services, 1991.

Grady, E. *The Portfolio Approach to Assessment.* Bloomington, Ind.: Phi Delta Kappa Educational Foundation, 1992.

Gregorc, A. *Style Delineator.* Maynard, Mass.: Gabriel Systems, 1982.

Guilford, J. *Way Beyond I.Q.* Buffalo, New York: Creative Education Foundation, 1988.

Harman, W. *The Global Mind Change: The Promise of the Last Years of the Twentieth Century.* Indianapolis: Knowledge Systems, Inc. 1988.

Harman, W., and H. Rheingold. *Higher Creativity: Liberating the Unconscious for Breakthrough Insights.* Los Angeles: J. P. Tarcher, 1985.

Harris, P. "Restructuring for Learning," *If Minds Matter: A Foreword to the Future,* vol. 1. Palatine, Ill.: IRI/Skylight Publishing, 1992, 3–11.

Hart, L. *Human Brain and Human Learning.* Village of Oak Creek, Ariz.: Books for Educators, 1983.

Hatch, T., and H. Gardner. "If Binet Had Looked beyond the Classroom: The Assessment of Multiple Intelligences," *International Journal of Educational Research* 14, no. 5, 415–29.

Herman, J. L. "What Research Tells Us about Good Assessment," *Educational Leadership* 49, no. 8 (May 1992): 74–78.

Herman, J. L., P. R. Aschbacher, and L. Winters. *A Practical Guide to Alternative Assessment.* Alexandria, Va.: Association for Supervision and Curriculum Development, 1992.

Houston, J. *Lifeforce: The Psycho-Historical Recovery of the Self.* New York: Delacorte Press, 1980.

———. *The Possible Human: A Course in Extending Your Physical, Mental, and Creative Abilities.* Los Angeles: J. P. Tarcher, 1982.

Kalick, B. *Changing Schools into Communities for Thinking.* Grand Forks, N. Dak.: University of North Dakota Press, 1989.

———. "Evaluation: A Collaborative Process," *If Minds Matter: A Foreword to the Future,* vol. 2. Palatine, Ill.: IRI/Skylight Publishing, 1992, 313–19.

Kovalick, S. *ITI: The Model. Integrated Thematic Instruction.* Village of Oak Creek, Ariz.: Susan Kovalik and Associates, 1993.

Kuhn, T. *The Structure of Scientific Revolutions.* Chicago: University of Chicago Press, 1962.

Lazear, David. *Seven Pathways of Learning: Teaching Students and Parents about Multiple Intelligences.* Tucson, Ariz.: Zephyr Press, 1993.

———. *Teaching for Multiple Intelligences.* Bloomington, Ind.: Phi Delta Kappa Educational Foundation, 1992.

———. *Seven Ways of Knowing: Teaching for Multiple Intelligences.* Palatine, Ill.: IRI/Skylight Publishing, 1991.

———. *Seven Ways of Teaching: The Artistry of Teaching with Multiple Intelligences.* Palatine, Ill.: IRI/Skylight Publishing, 1991.

———. "Multiple Intelligences and How We Nurture Them," *Cogitore* 4, no. 1 (Fall 1989):1, 4–5.

Majoy, P. *Doorways to Learning: A Model for Developing the Brain's Full Potential.* Tucson, Ariz.: Zephyr Press, 1993.

Meyer, C. "What's the Difference Between Authentic and Performance Assessment?" *Educational Leadership* 49, no. 8 (May 1992): 39–40.

Mitchell, R. *Testing for Learning: How New Approaches to Evaluation Can Improve American Schools.* New York: The Free Press, 1992.

Nuttall, D. L. "Performance Assessment: The Message from England," *Educational Leadership* 49, no. 8 (May 1992): 45–57.

O'Neil, J. "Putting Performance Assessment to the Test," *Educational Leadership* 49, no. 8 (May 1992): 14–19.

Oakes, J. *Keeping Track: How Schools Structure Inequality.* New Haven: Yale University Press, 1985.

Orlich, D. *Teaching Strategies.* Lexington, Mass.: D. C. Heath and Co., 1994.

Perkins, D. *Smart Schools.* New York: The Free Press, 1992.

Perkins, D., and G. Solomon. "Teaching for Transfer," *Educational Leadership* 46, no. 1 (1988): 22–32.

Perrone, V. *Expanding Student Assessment.* Alexandria, Va.: Association for Supervision and Curriculum Development, 1991.

Piaget, J. *The Psychology of Intelligence.* Totowa, N.J.: Littlefield Adams, 1972.

Schlechty, P. *Schools for the 21st Century.* San Francisco: Jossey-Bass, 1990.

Stefonek, T. *Alternative Assessment: A National Perspective: Policy Briefs.* Oak Brook, Ill.: North Central Regional Educational Laboratory, 1991.

Sternberg, R. "How Can We Teach Intelligence?" *Educational Leadership* 42, no. 1 (Sept. 1984): 38–48.

———"Thinking Styles: Keys to Understanding Student Performance," *Inquiry: Critical Thinking Across the Disciplines* 7, no. 3 (April 1991): 1, 32–38.

———. *Beyond I.Q.: A Triarchic Theory of Human Intelligence.* New York: Cambridge University Press, 1984.

———. *Intelligence Applied: Understanding and Increasing Your Intellectual Skills.* San Diego: Harcourt Brace Jovanovich, 1986.

Stiggins, R. "Assessment Literacy," *Phi Delta Kappan* 72, no. 7 (1991): 534–39.

———. "Revitalizing Classroom Assessment," *Phi Delta Kappan* 70, no. 5 (January 1988).

———. "Design and Development of Performance Assessments," *Educational Measurement: Issues and Practices.* National Council on Measurement in Education, 1987.

Stiggins, R., E. Rubel, and E. Quellmalz. *Measuring Thinking Skills in the Classroom: A Teacher's Guide.* Portland, Ore.: Northwest Regional Laboratory, 1986.

Ulrey, D., and J. Ulrey. "Developmentally Appropriate Practices Meet Multiple Intelligences," *Intelligences Connections* 2, no. 1 (1992): 4-6.

Wiggins, G. "Creating Tests Worth Taking," *Educational Leadership* 49, no. 8 (May 1992): 26-33.

———. "A True Test: Toward More Authentic and Equitable Assessment," *Phi Delta Kappan* 70, no. 9 (May 1989): 703-13.

———. "Rational Numbers: Toward Grading and Scoring that Helps Rather than Harms Learning." Article reprinted from the Coalition of Essential Schools, 1988.

———. "Standards, Not Standardization: Evoking Quality Student Work," *Educational Leadership* 48, no. 5 (February 1991): 18-25.

———. "Teaching to the (Authentic) Test," *Educational Leadership* 46, no. 7 (April 1989): 41-47.

Wolf, D. P., P. G. LeMahieu, and J. Eresh. "Good Measure: Assessment as a Tool for Educational Reform," *Educational Leadership* 49, no. 8 (May 1992): 8–13.

Worthen, B. R. "Critical Issues that Will Determine the Future of Alternative Assessment," *Phi Delta Kappan* 74, no. 6 (Feb. 1993): 444–56.

Worthen, B. R., and J. Sanders. *Educational Evaluation: Alternative Approaches and Practical Guidelines.* White Plains, New York: Longman, 1987.

NOTES

NOTES

NOTES

NOTES

NOTES

NOTES

NOTES

Help students tap their fullest potential—the MI way!

SEVEN PATHWAYS OF LEARNING
Teaching Students and Parents about Multiple Intelligences
by David Lazear
foreword by Arthur Costa
Grades K–12+

David Lazear dedicates this book to helping students tap their full learning potential.

Encourage your students to pass through four distinct levels of thinking about intelligence. You'll find 20 reproducible activities, 120 lesson extensions, personal reflection logs, and activities to involve parents. Each step encompasses a wider spiral of understanding.

1045-W . . . $35

INTELLIGENCE BUILDERS FOR EVERY STUDENT
44 Exercises to Expand MI in Your Classroom
by David Lazear
Grades 4–8

You'll find these activities excellent for self-discovery and developing classroom cohesiveness. Use this handy resource to build kinesthetic body awareness, linguistic humor, mathematical skills, group dynamics, and more!

1086-W . . . $25

MI IN ACTION
Your School and the Multiple Intelligences
in collaboration with David Lazear
Staff Development

Put these information-packed videos to work for you! Train the key players in your school about the basics of MI, then equip them with the complete set to give others an easy-to-understand overview. You'll be introduced to MI by leading experts: David Lazear, Nancy Margulies, Don Campbell, Anne Bruetsch, and others. You'll get these 5 videos—

1. **Getting the Picture: An Overview**
2. **A Creative Art: Teaching MI in the Elementary Grades**
3. **Tuning in the Learner: MI in Middle and High School Grades**
4. **Testing for Success: MI Assessment**
5. **Miss Ballou, Where Are You? An MI Guide for Parents**

Five 20-minute, full-color, VHS videotapes, and five 8–10 page accompanying booklets.

1705-W . . . $399

Get started with MI—it's easy with these handy resources!

TAP YOUR MULTIPLE INTELLIGENCES
Posters for the Classroom
text by David Lazear
illustrations by Nancy Margulies
Grades 3–12

Help your students use all their intelligences with full-size color posters. This handy set of 8 colorful posters will remind your students to use all 7 intelligences plus explore Howard Gardner's newest addition—the naturalist!

8 full-color posters, printed on lightweight poster board, each one 11" x 17".

1811-W . . . $25

STEP BEYOND YOUR LIMITS
Expanding Your MI Capacities
by David Lazear
Professional Development

Gain valuable insights and nurture your intelligences with a powerful learning tool designed for your development. Start by listening to a 40-minute tape packed with experiential activities and tips for awakening your MI capacities. Each tape has an accompanying workbook that leads you on a self-guided, step-by-step, capacity-building and enhancement program. The workbooks contain carefully designed exercises for helping you fully develop the distinct capacities related to each intelligence.

Eight 40-minute audiotapes and 7 workbooks: One tape on each intelligence and one overview tape; one workbook for each intelligence.

1914-W . . . $175

ORDER FORM ☎ Please include your phone number in case we have questions about your order.

Qty.	Item #	Title	Unit Price	Total
	1045-W	Seven Pathways of Learning	$35	
	1086-W	Intelligence Builders for Every Student	$25	
	1705-W	MI in Action	$399	
	1811-W	Tap Your Multiple Intelligences	$25	
	1914-W	Step Beyond Your Limits	$175	

Name _____

Address _____

City _____

State _____ Zip _____

Phone (_____) _____

Subtotal	
Sales Tax (AZ residents, 5%)	
S & H (10% of Subtotal, min.$3.00)	
Total (U.S. Funds only)	

CANADA: add 22% for S & H and G.S.T.

Method of payment (check one):

❏ Check or Money Order   ❏ Visa

❏ MasterCard   ❏ Purchase Order Attached

Credit Card No. _____

Expires _____

Signature _____

100% SATISFACTION GUARANTEE

Upon receiving your order you'll have 90 days of risk-free evaluation. If you are not 100% satisfied, return your order in saleable condition within 90 days for a 100% refund of the purchase price.

CALL, WRITE, OR FAX FOR YOUR FREE CATALOG!

To order write or call:

Zephyr Press®

REACHING THEIR HIGHEST POTENTIAL

P.O. Box 66006-W
Tucson, AZ 85728-6006

(520) 322-5090
FAX (520) 323-9402